Beginners' Spoken English & Grammar

Made Easy

Edited By,

DVNS Suresh

Written By,

SANJANA G. RAI

ISBN
Hardcase 979-8-89446-437-4
Paperback 979-8-89446-436-7

CONTENTS

SECTION A: GRAMMAR

Contents

SECTION B: SPOKEN ENGLISH

ACKNOWLEDGEMENTS

Creating this grammar book has been a journey filled with inspiration, hard work, and invaluable support from many individuals. I am deeply grateful to everyone who contributed to the successful completion of this project. First and foremost, I would like to express my heartfelt gratitude to my students, whose passion for language and dedication to education served as the driving force behind this book. I extend my sincere thanks to my loving uncle DVNS Suresh for his invaluable assistance in preparing the manuscript. Your insights and unwavering support have been instrumental in shaping this work. Your expertise, patience, and meticulous attention to detail have significantly enhanced the quality of this book. Additionally, I'm grateful to all the respective physical and digital resources which helped me boost my critical thinking and assisted me majorly design this book in a more simplified manner. A special mention goes to my family and friends for their constant encouragement and understanding during the many hours spent writing and revising. Your belief in me kept me motivated throughout this endeavour. Lastly, I am grateful to the Publisher for their professional guidance and support in bringing this book to publication. I'm thankful to all for your contributions, which have made this book a reality.

PREFACE

"This book is dedicated to all my dear students."

English being the Global and an international language, is extremely important in today's 21st century, as it allows in communication between different cultures and has significant importance in various aspects of life whether it may be personal or professional. In my book, I have designed the best data possible which will be great for beginners to start learning English effectively. My personal motive behind the creation of this book is the educational development of the students of rural areas and the beginners. Being an English teacher since years, I have come across various experiences up till now in my teaching career. Once I got an opportunity to teach Spoken English & Grammar to the students of rural areas. After stepping into it, I got to know the challenges faced by the students in rural areas regarding education especially when it comes to the subject of English. The educational scenario of the rural areas devastated me. Consequently, it motivated me to create this book for them as I think that this small step of mine would at least bring some development in the educational life of those students. My aim is to teach & develop the students of rural areas and make them capable enough to face and cope with the external world.

Besides, I'm very thankful to all my respective sources which helped me create this book. This book could be the best for beginners as it comprises of detailed explanation regarding every topic and contains a lot of practice exercises. First section of this book focuses on learning grammar and, the second section focuses on spoken English. Remember students, the key to master over anything is dedication, practice and self-study. Students of any age group above 5yrs could refer to this book. So, welcome to the world of simplified grammar.

"The development of my nation India, resides in the development of rural India", is what I strongly believe in.

SECTION A

GRAMMAR

GRAMMAR & ITS IMPORTANCE

What is Grammar?

Grammar is the backbone of language. It imparts a set of rules and principles that govern the structure, formation, and usage of words and sentences. It is a crucial aspect of communication, enabling us to convey meaning effectively and precisely.

Importance of Grammar in Communication

- **Clarity and Precision:** Grammar ensures that our thoughts and ideas are expressed clearly and precisely. Proper sentence structure, accurate word choices, and appropriate punctuation contribute to effective communication, reducing misunderstandings and ambiguity.

- **Enhanced Credibility:** Employing correct grammar enhances credibility and professionalism. Good grammar indicates attention and respect for the language, instilling confidence in the speaker or writer.

- **Writing Skills:** Grammar plays a crucial role in developing strong writing skills. It helps students convey their ideas coherently, structure their arguments logically, and produce well-organized and grammatically correct essays, reports, and research papers.

- **Reading and Comprehension:** Understanding grammar aids in reading comprehension. Knowledge of grammar enables students to identify sentence structures, recognize parts of speech, and comprehend the intended meaning of texts.

- **Language Proficiency:** Mastery of grammar is essential for language proficiency. It enables students to communicate fluently and accurately, facilitating their ability to express themselves effectively in both written and spoken forms.

- **Business Communication:** Proper grammar is crucial in professional communication. Whether it's writing emails, reports, or presentations, using correct grammar instils professionalism and ensures that the message is conveyed clearly and effectively.

- **Job Prospects:** A strong command of grammar is often considered a prerequisite in many job positions. Employers value employees who can communicate effectively, write error-free documents, and uphold the standards of the organization.

- **Academic and Research Fields:** In academic and research domains, accurate grammar is vital for publishing papers, presenting findings, and collaborating with colleagues. Precise grammar ensures that ideas are communicated accurately and professionally.

- **Speaking Skills:** Learning English grammar enhances speaking proficiency. It equips learners with the knowledge of sentence structures, vocabulary usage, and grammar rules necessary for fluent and accurate oral communication.

- **Academic Advancement:** English grammar proficiency is crucial for academic success. It facilitates understanding and analysis of complex texts, allows for effective participation in discussions and debates, and enhances the quality of written assignments.

- **Professional Growth:** In today's global job market, English language skills are highly valued. Knowledge of English grammar opens up career opportunities in multinational companies, international organizations, and industries where English is the primary language of communication.

- **Cultural Exchange and Travel:** Learning English grammar enables individuals to engage in cross-cultural communication. It facilitates interactions with people from diverse backgrounds, enhances travel experiences, and promotes a deeper understanding of different cultures.

- Mastering English grammar is essential for effective communication, language proficiency, and personal growth. It empowers individuals to express themselves accurately and clearly, enhances their reading and writing skills, and expands opportunities in education and the professional realm.

- Learning English grammar facilitates cultural exchange, travel experiences, and a deeper understanding of diverse perspectives. Moreover, it nurtures cognitive skills, critical thinking, and a profound appreciation for the English language. By dedicating time and effort to learning English grammar, individuals can unlock their potential for effective communication, academic success, and personal development in today's interconnected world.

- Grammar forms the foundation of effective communication, influencing clarity, comprehension, and professionalism. By adhering to grammar rules, individuals can express their thoughts clearly, minimize misunderstandings, and enhance their credibility.

- In educational settings, grammar plays a crucial role in developing strong writing skills, aiding reading comprehension, and fostering language proficiency.

- Moreover, in professional environments, proper grammar is essential for maintaining a polished image and facilitating effective business communication. Recognizing the importance of grammar and striving for accuracy and clarity can significantly enhance one's ability to communicate and succeed in various personal, educational, and professional endeavours.

02

ARTICLES

VOWELS: a,e,i,o,u.

CONSONANTS: All the other letters except vowels.

A and **AN** are **indefinite articles**. The difference depends on the sound at the beginning of the next word. A and AN are **used with singulars only**.

When the next word starts with a CONSONANT sound, we use 'A' before that word. Ex: a dog, a tree, a car, a book, a zoo, etc.

When the next word starts with a VOWEL sound, we use 'AN' before that word. Ex: an apple, an elephant, an ice cube, an orange, an umbrella, etc.

Note: The sound of the letter is important.

Ex: (i) a <u>h</u>ouse BUT an <u>h</u>our

Here, '**H**' at the beginning of the '**hour**' is silent, the pronounciation of hour is 'aauhrr', which starts with vowel sound 'aa', so we use 'an' before hour.

(ii) an <u>u</u>ncle BUT a <u>u</u>niverse

Here, '**U**' at the beginninng of the '**universe**' sounds like 'YOU', which starts with the consonant sound 'y', so we use 'a' before universe.

[For a better understanding, one can refer to the **'Swar' and 'Vyanjan'** in the Hindi Grammar. **'Swar' are the vowels and 'Vyanjan' are the**

consonants. The English words starting with sound of Swar are applied 'AN', while the words starting with the sound of a Vyanjan are applied 'A'.]

A, AN

'A' **and** *'AN'* are known as **indefinite articles.**

A- used with **consonant** sounds.

AN- used with **vowel** sounds.

Uses of Indefinite articles.

1] It is used in the numerical sense of one.

Ex: Not **a** single student attended the class today, I didn't see **an** apple in the basket.

2] To say what kind of thing or person something or somebody is.

Ex: What **a** sophisticated lady!, Rahul is **an** intelligent student.

3] With the names of professions and occupations.

Ex: My sister is **a** doctor, My mother is **a** homemaker.

4] Use before singular nouns.

Ex: India is **a** country, Harvard is **a** university.

THE

'The' is known as a **definite article.** It can be **used with both singular (specific) and plural** words. We use 'The' when we talk about a particular person, place, or a thing or anything already referred to.

1] Something that is unique or only one.

Ex: The Sun, The Earth

2] Geographical places.

- Rivers: The Ganges, The Yamuna.
- Mountain ranges: The Himalayas, The Andes.
- Deserts: The Sahara, The Thar.
- Oceans and seas: The Pacific, The Atlantic.
- Groups of islands: The Lakshadweep, The Andaman.
- Some countries: The USA, The Netherlands.
- Points on the globe: The Equator, The North Pole.
- Geographical areas: The Middle East, The South Asia.

3] The second time you talk about the same noun.

Ex: I bought **a car. The car** is Mercedes.

4] Directions (cardinal points)

Ex: The north-west/ the east/ the south.

5] With the heads of office.

Ex: The Prime Minister, The Principal

6] When a singular noun represents a whole class.

Ex: The Rose is the King of the flowers; The Giraffe is the tallest animal.

7] Before the surnames to indicate family.

Ex: The Jaiswals (Jaiswal family), The Singhs (Singh family)

8] With the superlatives.

Ex: Mt. Everest is the *highest* peak, The shark is the *biggest* mammal on Earth.

9] Used with abstract nouns.

Ex: The beauty, the care, the kindness, the love, etc.

10] With the names of religious books.

Ex: The Gita, The Bible, The Quran, The Guru Granth Sahib

11] With the periodicals.

Ex: The Hindu Times, The Indian Express, The New York Times

Note: Pronunciations- Spelling of 'THE' is always the same but it differs in pronunciations.

'THE' is used for words starting with consonant sounds.

'THEEEE' is used for words starting with vowel sounds.

NO ARTICLE

When you talk about any category or group in general, use 'no article'. However, we use 'no article' in other situations without grammatical rules.

Use 'no article' before:

- Names of languages: Hindi, Mandarin, Spanish, Prakrit, Tamil
- Nationalities: Indian, Italian, African, Mexican (unless referring to the population of the place e.g. 'The Indians are known for their spicy food.').
- Names of sports: Hockey, Badminton, Cricket.
- Names of subjects: Politics, Economics, History, Mathematics.

When it comes to geographical places, there aren't any rules to help you here – you just have to familiarise yourself with the ones that need 'the' or not.

Do NOT use 'the' before:

- Lakes: Dal Lake, Wular Lake
- Mountains: Mount Everest, Mount Abu.
- Continents: Asia, Antarctica, North America

- Most countries: Belgium, Switzerland.
- States/provinces/regions: Maharashtra, Karnataka, Kashmir.
- Cities, towns, villages: London, Nagpur, Nashik.
- Islands: Bali, Cuba, Greenland.
- Street names: 2nd Avenue, RBI Square

EXERCISE 1

Q1] Fill in the blanks with a, an, or the.

1] _____ tent   2] _____ arm   3] _____ lemon   4] _____ magazine

5] _____ eye   6] _____ eraser   7] _____ uniform   8] _____ ring

9] _____ rabbit   10] _____ x-ray   11] _____ ear   12] _____ love

13] _____ banana   14] _____ orange   15] _____ igloo   16] _____ ambulance

17] _____ lion   18] _____ giraffe   19] _____ umbrella   20] _____ apple

21] _____ fox   22] _____ ox   23] _____ cube   24] _____ artist

25] _____ old man   26] _____ leaf   27] _____ spider   28] _____ black dog

29] _____ hour   30] _____ herb   31] _____ shark   32] _____ icy winter

33] _____ beauty   34] _____ teacher   35] _____ house   36] _____ zoo

37] _____ care   38] _____ office   39] _____ garden   40] _____ childhood

EXERCISE 2

Q2] A) Fill in the blanks with a, an, the.

1] I saw _____ old bike. 2] I climbed _____ tree. 3] The spider ate _____ ant. 4] That lady has _____ beautiful bird. 5] It is _____ pretty dress. 6] _____ elephants are very big animals. 7] _____ lion is the king of the jungle. 8] This is _____ interesting book. 9] My mother is _____ surgeon. 10] _____ Delhi city is the capital of India. 11] India is _____ beautiful country.

12] _____ rabbits are faster than _____ tortoises. 13] I have _____ bag of wheat. 14] _____ well is full of water. 15] _____ Khans are invited to the ceremony.

Q2] B) Fill articles in the following:

1] Will you come to _____ seminar next Sunday? 2] I bought _____ new microwave. 3] I think _____ woman over there is jealous of you. 4] I watched _____ movie you asked me to watch. 5] She was wearing _____ fashionable dress. 6] I love reading _____ mythological books. 7] She is _____ careless girl. 8] Do you want to go to _____ garden where we first met? 9] He is _____ magician. 10] I want to go to _____ most fascinating place.

EXERCISE 3

Q3] A) Tick the correct article:

1. Amisha wanted to read a / an thrilling book. 2. The class went on a / an educational trip. 3. He likes to read an / the short stories. 4. Avoni put a / an orange on her yogurt. 5. My friend likes making an / the cake. 6. The bear caught a / an stick. 7. I saw a / an owl at the zoo. 8. I quickly ate the / an muffins. 9. A / an oval is shaped like a / an egg. 10. Rama has a / an gorgeous dress.

Q3] B) Circle the correct article:

1. He carried a/an axe. 2. My mom poured lemonade from a/an pitcher. 3. That cat is stuck in a/an tree. 4. A/an elephant has a long trunk. 5. The SUV was driving down a/an dirty road. 6. There is a/an chair at the table. 7. Elena ate a/an egg for breakfast. 8. Tom runs as fast as a/an cheetah. 9. There is a/an inky spot on my pants. 10. I love to read a/an book.

EXERCISE 4

Q4] Read each sentence carefully, circle the error and right the correct article.

1. We always go for skating on an lake in the winter._______________

2. My mom put a burgers in an oven._______________

3. The tree in an garden grew tall._______________

4. The Amazon rainforest is an dangerous place._______________

5. The big brown bear is an most hairy one._______________

6. I like the pictures in an frame._______________

7. The math problems were an hard one to do._______________

8. The movie we watched was an fantastic one._______________

9. My uncle ran to an store for the item._______________

10. There were many kids in an sandbox at the park._______________

Q5] Fill in the blanks with the articles a, an, the.

1] Iron is _____ useful metal.   2] He is not _____ honorable man.

3] You are _____ fool to say that.   4] Honest people speak _____ truth.

5] Do you see _____ blue sky?   6] Aladdin had _____ magical lamp.

7] _____ reindeer is a native of Norway.   8] _____ sun shines brightly.

9] _____ lion is _____ king of beasts.   10] He returned after _____ hour.

Q6] Fill in the blanks with the articles a, an, the.

1] _____ cheetah runs _____ fastest.   2] Man is _____ rational being.

3] He read _____ book I gave him.   4] He can play upon _____ flute very well.

5] _____ topic we are discussing, is very interesting.   6] He is _____ M.Sc.

7] _____ stars are shining in _____ sky.   8] We saw _____ snake in _____ grass.

9] I have read _____ Arabian Nights.   10] I saw _____ boy running.

11] _____ whole oil was spilled.   12] I saw _____ old lady in _____ street.

13] _____ higher you go, _____ cooler it is.   14] He came here _____ hour ago.

15] _____ handle of this mug is durable.   16] She gave me _____ magazine.

17] The Hitavada is _____ English paper.   18] All _____ players were present.

19] _____ less you work, _____ less you gain.   20] He is _____ Italian boy.

Q7] Fill in the blanks with the articles a, an, the:

1] I have _____ bag of barley.   2] _____ river is full of water.

3] We rode _____ elephant.   4] He hit himself with _____ stick.

5] _____ rich old lady bought _____ beautiful necklace.

6] _____ trip was very nice.   7] Can I ask you _____ question?

8] You look very tired. You need _____ break.

9] Catherine is in _____ bathroom.

10] Bonnie is _____ interesting person. You must meet her.

EXERCISE 4

Q8] Fill in the blanks with the articles a, an, the:

1] Spanish is _____ easy language.   2] Mumbai is _____ best place to live in.

3] She is _____ untidy girl.   4] I bought _____ horse, _____ ox, and _____ buffalo.

5] If you see him, give him _____ message.   6] The guide knows _____ way.

7] Let us discuss _____ matter seriously. 8] Man is _____ wonderful animal.

9] India is one of _____ most industrial countries in Asia.

10] She is _____ honor to this profession.

Q9] Put a, an & the wherever necessary in the following sentences.

1] My friend is _____ M.A. in mathematics.

2] Mumbai is _____ London of India.

3] We are going to _____ cinema.   4] I know how to play _____ ukulele.

5] I have got _____ headache.   6] _____ Ganga is _____ holy river.

7] _____ Quran is read by _____ Muslims.   8] Damon is _____ unique boy.

9] He is _____ most intelligent boy in the class.

10] Yesterday I met _____ European playing with _____ boy.

EXERCISE 5

Q10] Fill in the Blanks with appropriate indefinite articles 'a' or 'an'.

1. ...... old man met me last week. 2. Paul built ...... yard for his cattle. 3. She ate only ...... orange for her breakfast. 4. My grandmother told me ...... story of Jesus Christ. 5. Mr.Bansod bought ...... new car. 6. My son is ...... Ph.D from Agra University. 7. Raman is ...... intelligent son of ...... poor tailor. 8. Anjali lodged ...... F.I.R. against the cheat. 9. Pass me ...... slice of bread. 10. Vaishnavi has gone on ...... month's vacation. 11. Malkanpur is ...... small village. 12. Visitors can meet the patient only twice ...... day. 13. There was ...... buffalo in the field. 14. Shanan made ...... error of judgement. 15. He was late by ...... hour for the meeting. 16. Anurag has ...... interest in acting. 17. Nihal's brother is ...... engineer in ...... reputed company. 18. There is ...... eucalyptus tree near my house. 19. She is ...... honorary secretary of the club. 20. We met ...... European girl in Coorg.

EXERCISE 6

Q11] Fill in the blanks with the articles a, an, the :

1] Germany is _____ European country.

2] Elephant is _____ vegetarian animal.

3] I must go to see _____ old teacher.

4] I want _____ kiwi from that basket.

5] _____ church on the corner _____ so large.

6] _____ professor is late today.

7] I borrowed _____ pencil from your pouch.

8] I am _____ university student.

9] Please give me _____ cake that is on the table.

10] I lived on _____ Central Street when I was 5yrs old.

11] She goes to _____ temple in _____ mornings.

12] I bought _____ umbrella to go out in _____ rain.

13] Kiran is _____ best student in the class.

14] _____ camel is _____ ship of the desert.

15] This book has won _____ Booker prize.

16] Harishchandra was _____ honest king.

17] _____ ink in my pen is red.

18] Our neighbors has _____ cow & _____ dog.

19] She returned after _____ couple of hours.

20] There is _____ institution for _____ blind, _____ deaf & _____ dumb in this city.

Q12] Fill in the Blanks with appropriate indefinite articles 'a' or 'an'.

1] Excuse me, can you tell me how to get to _____ city centre?

2] Shall we go out for _____ supper this evening? Yes, that is _____ good idea.

3] It is _____ nice day. Let us go for _____ walk.

4] Katerina is _____ student. When she finishes her studies, she wants to be _____ journalist.

5] Caroline lives with two friends in _____ flat near _____ college where she is studying. _____ flat is small but she likes it.

6] Sahil and Vishakha have got two children, _____ boy and _____ girl. _____ boy is ten years old and _____ girl is three.

7] Aamir works in _____ factory. Harsh has not got _____ job at the moment.

8] _____ man and _____ woman were sitting opposite to me. _____ man was American but I think _____ woman was British.

9] I met _____ boy in the store. _____ was Scottish.

10] Gold is _____ precious metal. It is used in _____ jewelry.

Q13] Fill in the Blanks with appropriate articles:

1. ...... village chief has started ...... utensil shop. 2. Avighna's father is ...... principal of our college. 3. ...... Ganges flows from ...... Himalayas. 4. Please give me ...... copy of The Times of India. 5. ...... Jaiswals are particularly interested in music. 6. ...... market will remain closed for ...... week. 7. She wrote ...... paper for ...... seminar. 8. Rohini bought ...... cup of coffee. 9. ...... earth moves round ...... sun. 10. He met with ......accident yesterday. 11. Neetu saw......cat in ...... garden. 12. We saw ...... crocodile in ...... zoo. 13. Khushboo's father is ...... advocate in ...... district court. 14. Gopal is ...... tallest boy in ...... class. 15. She gave me ...... call in the

evening. 16. Dr.Tejaswini is ...... Urdu teacher. 17. I met ...... boy. ...... boy was very polite. 18. Reading is ...... good habit. 19. He is ...... captain in ...... army. 20. Mr. Zade is ...... honorary president of our society.

<u>EXERCISE 7</u>

Q14] Fill in the blanks with the articles.

1. There is _____ lizard on _____ roof.   2. I bought _____ laptop yesterday.

3. She is waiting for _____ Uber.   4. You should consult _____ doctor.

5. I am reading _____ magazine.   6. We are waiting for _____ results.

7. She told me _____ lie.   8. I brought home _____ love birds last week.

9. If you are hungry, you can eat _____ custard apple.

10. _____ mangoes I bought yesterday were very sweet.

Q15] Fill in the blanks with appropriate articles.

1. We have _____ beautiful garden. _____ garden is full of roses.

2. Is polo _____ popular sport in _____ world? No, it isn't.

3. I'd like _____ glass of litchi juice, please.

4. Can you give me _____ envelope, please? Oh! Where's _____ envelope?

5. Is there _____ police station near here?

6. Camels live in _____ desert.

7. My brother is in _____ USA.

8. Would you like _____ hamburger?

9. Sana has got _____ cat. What is _____ cat's name?

10. _____ hall is very cold. Hasn't it got _____ central heating system?

EXERCISE 8

Q16] Add articles in the blanks:

1] Shanan wants _____ little more sugar.

2] My mother gave a cotton candy to _____ child who was crying.

3] Diamond is _____ expensive stone.

4] We visited _____ Taj Mahal two years back.

5] This job will provide you with _____ opportunity to show your talent and knowledge.

6] _____ animals at the zoo are not fed well.

7] While working in _____ factory, I saw _____ beggar sleeping on _____ footpath.

8] Fatima wants to become _____ air hostess, but her family wants her to be _____ IPS officer.

9] I have read _____ Vedas and _____ Puranas.

10] Twelve inches make _____ foot.

11] _____ Sun is shining today but tonight it is not certain whether _____ moon will shine or not

12] _____ Sun rises in the East and sets in the West.

13] The boy in _____ lavender T-shirt is my brother.

14] _____ moon does not shine in _____ daytime.

15] Draw _____ map of Tamil Nadu.

16] It is _____ honor to be here at your commencement ceremony.

17] Who does not want to live in _____ open air?

18] _____ brave always does brave things.

19] My grandmother gave me _____ brand new bike.

20] She has _____ interesting book on leadership.

03

SINGULAR AND PLURAL

One

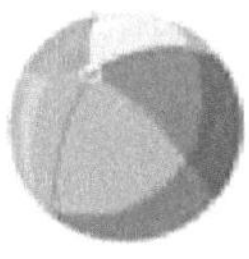

Singular

More Than One

Plural

SINGULAR AND PLURAL NOUNS WITH RULES

Rule 1: For regular nouns, **add '-s'** while converting in the plural form.

Ex: house-houses, car-cars, apple-apples, table-tables

Rule 2: For words ending in **S, CH, SH, X or Z**, add '**-es**'.

Ex: box-boxes, ben**ch**-benches, wa**sh**-washes, bu**s**-buses

Rule 3: For words ending in **F** or **FE**, add '**-ves**' after removing F/FE.

Ex: wolf-wolves, knife-knives, life-lives, leaf-leaves

Note: There are few exceptions in this case, like roof-roofs, cliff-cliffs.

Rule 4: For words ending with **VOWEL+Y, add '-s'**.

Ex: donkey-donkeys, guy-guys, key-keys, boy-boys.

Rule 5: For words ending with **CONSONANT+Y, add '-ies'** after removing **Y**.

Ex: city-cities, country-countries, party-parties

Rule 6: For words ending with **VOWEL+O, add '-s'**.

Ex: zoo-zoos, kangaroo-kangaroos, radio-radios, video-videos

Rule 7: For words ending with **CONSONANT+O, add '-es'**.

Ex: echo-echoes, hero-heroes, tomato-tomatoes, potato-potatoes

Note: There are some exceptions like, piano-pianos, photo-photos.

Rule 8: Irregular nouns are changed in a different manner.

Ex: Person – people, Ox – oxen, Man – men, Woman – women, Caveman – cavemen, Policeman – policemen, Child – children, Tooth – teeth, Foot – feet, Goose – geese, Mouse – mice.

Note: Some nouns have no change.

Ex: 1 sheep- 5 sheep, 1 deer- 2 deer, 1 series- 10 series, 1 species- 2 species.

EXERCISE 9

SINGULAR VS PLURAL NOUNS

Q17] Underline the noun and write "S" if it is singular or "P" if it is plural.

1) Put your clothes away. ___________________

2) Your boots are dirty! ___________________

3) The bear is lazy. ___________________

4) We will buy four tickets. ___________________

5) Children, please sit down. ___________________

6) Where is my book? _______________________

7) Your socks are red. _______________________

8) There is one person missing. _______________________

9) Clean your room. _______________________

10) Take off your boots please. _______________________

11) You will need a hat. _______________________

12) Do you want the lights on? _______________________

13) These pencils are sharp. _______________________

14) Meera has the eraser. _______________________

15) Write three sentences. _______________________

16) Let's read this book. _______________________

17) Play with the blocks. _______________________

18) Put your toys away. _______________________

19) Do you have a marker? _______________________

20) I can share my sandwich with you. _______________________

21) Are all the vehicles turning around? _______________________

22) Can you get the eggs please? _______________________

23) Can you pet the dog? _______________________

24) Count the glasses please. _______________________

25) We need one more fork. _______________________

26) There are birds in there. _______________________

27) The car will not start. _______________________

28) You have a new bicycle. _______________________

29) These kittens were born recently. _______________________

30) I count only two cushions. _______________________

EXERCISE 10

MAKING NOUNS PLURAL

Q18] Write the plural nouns for each.

NOTE: We add -es to the plural of singular nouns that end in ch, sh, s, x and z.

[A] Write the plural words: Add "s" or "es".

1) drum _______________   2) pin _______________

3) bird _______________   4) shirt _______________

5) dish _______________   6) spoon _______________

7) fork _______________   8) box _______________

9) sandwich _______________   10) brick _______________

11) medicine _______________   12) chair _______________

13) desk _______________   14) truck _______________

15) car _______________   16) tree _______________

17) ant _______________   18) fox _______________

19) dog _______________   20) rabbit _______________

[B] Write the plural words: Add "s" or "es".

1) pool _______________   2) deck _______________

3) ditch _______________   4) road _______________

5) street _______________   6) lake _______________

7) peach _______________   8) heart _______________

9) window _______________   10) wall _______________

11) station _______________   12) house _______________

13) building _____________   14) church _____________

15) mall _____________   16) apartment _____________

17) sea _____________   18) beach _____________

19) bridge _____________   20) waltz _____________

21) dance _____________   22) sport _____________

23) gas _____________   24) clutch _____________

EXERCISE 11

NOUNS ENDING IN 'y'

Q19] Add 'ies': When a noun ends in 'y', we add 'ies' to its plural.

For example: one story, many stories.

[A] Write the plural words.

firefly _____________   hobby _____________   cherry _____________

country _____________   trophy _____________   belly _____________

puppy _____________   sky _____________   library _____________

bully _____________   activity _____________   daisy _____________

butterfly _____________   froggy _____________   party _____________

enemy _____________   story _____________   pony _____________

family _____________   city _____________   bunny _____________

spy _____________   penny _____________   fly _____________

army _____________   body _____________   berry _____________

baby _____________   factory _____________   lady _____________

NOUNS ENDING IN VOWEL PLUS 'Y'

Q20] Write the plural of singular nouns that end in a 'vowel + y'.

When a singular noun ends in a vowel and 'y', such as in 'toy', we just add an s to its plural: 'toys'.

[A] Write the plural words.

1) toy __________   2) ploy ________   3) play _________

4) blue jay _______   5) birthday ________   6) alley ________

7) tray ________   8) turkey ________   9) monkey ________

10) valley ________

[B] Write the plural words.

1) day __________   2) chimney ________   3) donkey ________

4) delay ________   5) key _________   6) essay _________

7) joy _________   8) way _________   9) survey _______

10) guy ________

[C] Write the plural words.

1) attorney _______   2) play _________   3) stay _________

4) volley ________   5) driveway ________   6) highway ________

7) kidney ________   8) hallway ________   9) holiday ________

10) relay ________

EXERCISE 12

IRREGULAR PLURAL NOUNS

There are hundreds of Irregular plural nouns are nouns that do **not** become plural by adding -s or es at the end of the word, such as *flower - flowers*. In these exercises students have to match each singular noun with its irregular plural noun.

Q21] [A] Match the singular and plural nouns.

man	mice
child	teeth
deer	men
leaf	fish
wolf	children
mouse	deer
fish	wolves
tooth	leaves

[B] Match the singular and plural nouns.

woman	feet
foot	oxen
knife	geese
goose	women
sheep	cacti
moose	knives
cactus	sheep
ox	moose

[C] Match the singular and plural nouns.

person	calves
fungus	series
tuna	people
basis	shelves

criterion	fungi
shelf	bases
calf	tuna
series	criteria

EXERCISE 13

WRITING IRREGULAR PLURAL NOUNS

There are hundreds of irregular plural nouns that students will have to memorize. In this exercise, complete the sentences with the plural irregular noun indicated in its singular form.

Q22] Complete the sentences with the irregular plural noun forms of the word in brackets.

[A] 1) The ___________ ran to the playground. (child)

2) Your ___________ have grown; you need new sandals. (foot)

3) Many ___________ will attend the conference. (person)

4) Books go on the ___________. (shelf)

5) We are having ___________ tonight. (tuna)

6) The farmer's cow had two ___________. (calf)

7) We discussed the business ___________ together. (criterion)

8) The panel had mainly ___________ in it. (man)

9) Trees lose their ___________ in the fall. (leaf)

10) I could hear the ___________ howling last night. (wolf)

[B] Complete the sentences with the plural form of the word in brackets.

1) The ___________ go beside the spoons. (knife)

2) There are trillions of ___________ in this ocean. (fish)

3) The ___________ flew south for winter. (goose)

4) The ___________ went shopping. (woman)

5) Don't water the ___________ too much. (cactus)

6) Two ___________ are needed to pull the cart. (ox)

7) Brush your ___________ before going to bed. (tooth)

8) I think there are ___________ in the house. (mouse)

9) Look at the ___________ in the forest! (deer)

10) Those are interesting ___________. (fungus)

[C] Complete the sentences with the plural form of the word in brackets.

1) Place all your ___________ in a jar. (penny)

2) There are so many ___________. (box)

3) I like the pattern of the ___________. (series)

4) What are the ___________ of your conclusion? (basis)

5) The ___________ are eating the grass. (sheep)

6) How many ___________ were there? (moose)

7) The steel and iron ___________ are sharp. (knife)

8) She was telling the ___________ a fairy tale. (child)

9) Are your ___________ cold? (foot)

10) Put two ___________ together to get a whole. (half)

04

PARTS OF SPEECH

The part of speech indicates that how the word functions in meaning as well as grammatically within the sentence. There are eight parts of speech. For learning the basic spoken English, the parts of speech are the only requirement that's why known as 'Parts of Speech'. A sentence cannot be formed without their help. They are as follows:

[1] **<u>NOUN</u>:** Name of a thing, a person, an animal, a place, or an idea.

Examples: Nikhil, India, Lion, laptop, honesty, etc.

[2] **<u>PRONOUN</u>**: A pronoun is used in place of a noun or noun phrase to avoid repetition.

Examples: I, he, she, you, it, we, us, them, herself, etc.

[3] **<u>ADJECTIVE</u>**: Describes, modifies or gives more information about a noun or pronoun.

Examples: Yellow, loyal, young, five, German, etc.

[4] **<u>VERB</u>**: Shows an action or a state of being. It can show what someone is doing or did.

Examples: go, speaking, lived, been, is, etc.

[5] **<u>ADVERB</u>**: Modifies a verb, an adjective or another adverb. It tells how (often), where, when.

Examples: slowly, very, always, well, etc.

[6] <u>PREPOSITION</u>: Shows the relationship of a noun, noun phrase or pronoun to another word.

Examples: at, on, in, from, with, about, etc.

[7] <u>CONJUNCTION</u>: Joins two words, ideas, phrases together and shows how they are connected.

Examples: or, but, and, because, until, if, etc.

[8] <u>INTERJECTION</u>: A word or phrase that expresses a strong emotion. It is a short exclamation.

Examples: Ouch!, Wow!, Hey!, Oh!, Ugh!, Sshh!

[All the parts of speech are explained in detail further.]

NOUNS

What is a noun?

A noun is a word that is used to identify or classify a person, place, animal, thing or idea.

➤ There are six types of nouns. They are as follows:

[1] **PROPER NOUN:** It is used to name a specific (or individual) person, place or thing. Proper nouns start with a capital letter.

Ex: Shrushti, Nagpur, Saturn, India, Shreyash, etc.

[2] **COMMON NOUN:** It is used to name people, places or things in general. It refers to the class or type of person on thing (without being specific).

Ex: boy, woman, animal, car, city, state, etc.

<u>**DIFFERENCE BETWEEN**</u>
<u>**PROPER NOUN AND COMMON NOUN**</u>

COMMON NOUNS	PROPER NOUNS
They don't have a name.	They have a name.
Car	Mercedes
Ocean	Indian ocean
Singer	Mickle Jackson

Chocolate	Bournville
Biscuit	Bourbon
Country	Europe
Laptop	Lenovo

[3] COLLECTIVE NOUN: It refers to a set or group of people, animals or things. They are often followed by OF+PLURAL NOUN.

Ex: bouquet of flowers, collection of stamps, team of players, army of soldiers, etc.

[4] CONCRETE NOUN (MATERIAL NOUN): It refers to people or things that exist physically and that at least one of the senses (among the five senses) can detect.

Ex: cat, tree, flower, mango, saree, etc.

[5] ABSTRACT NOUN: It has no physical existence. They refer to ideas, emotions and concepts you cannot see, touch, hear, smell or taste.

Ex: time, happiness, bravery, courage, freedom, love, etc.

[6] COMPOUND NOUN: When two or more words come together to create a noun. They can be written as one word, joined by a hyphen or written as separate words.

Ex: Sister-in-law, tea table, table lamp, etc.

> ➤ The nouns are further classified into **countable and uncountable nouns.**

COUNTABLE NOUN: They can be counted. They have a singular and a plural form and can be used with a number or a/an before it. They are sometimes called Count nouns.

Ex: bike, table, cup, girl, a few books, a lot of oranges, etc.

UNCOUNTABLE NOUN: They cannot be counted. They often refer to substances, liquids, and abstract ideas. They are sometimes called Mass nouns.

Ex: milk, water, air, wood, care, hatred, etc.

➢ Gender nouns can be categorized into **masculine gender, feminine gender, common gender and neuter gender.**

Masculine Gender: Denotes a male person or animal.
Ex: boy, grandfather, lion, tiger, father, nephew, etc.

Feminine Gender: Denotes a female person or animal.
Ex: girl, grandmother, lioness, tigress, mother, niece, etc.

Common Gender: Denotes either a male or a female.
Ex: cousin, baby, kid, child, neighbor, orphan, etc.

Neuter Gender: Denotes things without life or gender.
Ex: fan, broom, table, box, house, pen, etc.

[Extra vocabulary, for reference, and learning.]

Collective nouns List:

A band of musicians, a board of directors, a choir of singers, a class of students, a crowd of people, a gang of thieves, a pack of thieves, a panel of experts, a team of players, a troupe of dancers, an army of ants, a flock of birds, a flock of sheep, a herd of deer, a hive of bees, a litter of puppies, a pack of wolves, a school of fish, a team of horses, a pride of lions, a bouquet of flowers, a bunch of flowers, a fleet of ships, a forest of trees, a galaxy of stars, a pack of cards, a pack of lies, a pair of shoes, a range of mountains, a wad of notes, belt of asteroids, a bunch of keys, a bundle of sticks, a catalogue of prices, a chest of drawers, a cluster of coconuts, fleet of vehicles, a reel of film.

Abstract Nouns List:

Belief, Sorrow, Joy, Failure, Slavery, Riches, Fashion, Envy, Success, Fear, Union, Luxury, Freedom, Generosity, Wit, Peace, Hatred, Thrill, Care, Wealth, Religion, Divorce, Goal, Stupidity, Friendship, Goodness, Timing, Appetite, Loneliness, Pleasure, Love, Beauty, Annoyance,

Kindness, Nap, Gain, Talent, Lie, Truth, Solitude, Justice, Bravery, Calm, Childhood, Confusion, Ability, Loss, Thought, Growth, Cleverness, Anger, Horror, Marriage, Delay, Philosophy, Generation, Wisdom, Dishonesty, Happiness, Coldness, Poverty, Brilliance, Awareness, Idea, Disregard, Irritation, Advantage, Mercy, Speed, Pain, Gossip, Crime, Comfort, Life, Patience, Deceit, Elegance.

GERUND

A gerund, sometimes called a verbal noun, is a noun formed from a verb. Since all gerunds end in *-ing*, they are sometimes confused as being a verb (present participle).

Example: *Running is good for you.*

Here *running* looks like a verb because of its *-ing* ending but it is a noun (gerund) because we are talking about the concept of running, we are talking about a thing.

Examples of gerunds: reading, writing, dancing, thinking, etc.

EXERCISE 14

IDENTIFYING AND USING NOUNS

Q23] A) Identify the Nouns and circle them.

Happy pillow goat make boy desk box up fast lamp kite song dance Jug water pencil book draw snow eat slow towel sky monkey girl throw sun bat hit not too fat ball dad tree mat cap run to day book hook that arm game hat but foot Ganga sad

B) Complete the sentences using the nouns given below:

(brother, chairs, flowers, backyard, sitar, Paul, dog, pasta, friend, uncle, table)

1. I like to eat _________.   2.My pet is a _________.

3. I play the ___________.   4. There are six ___________ at our ___________.

5. The ___________ smell so good in the ___________.   6. Your ___________ is tall!

7. This is my ___________. His name is ___________.

Q24](A) Circle the nouns.

Log   work   novel   leave   bulb   tree   find   pick   Blanket
help   Samosa   bear   want   sun

(B) Complete the sentences using nouns from above.

1. Dad turned on the _______________ because it was dark.

2. His pet _______________ scares me.

3. _______________ is my favorite food.

4. The _______________ keeps me warm.

5. I finished reading my _______________.

6. The _______________ is very bright in the sky.

EXERCISE 15

Q25] (A) Circle the nouns in each sentence:

1. The car is parked in the garage.   2. Litchis are delicious.

3. There is sand on the beach.   4. My hamster is fuzzy.

5. The jet is very fast.

(B) Write a sentence using a person and two places.

____

(C) Write a sentence using an animal & a thing.

____

Q26] (A) Circle the nouns in each sentence:

1. The picture is of volcanoes.   2. Shelves hold books and toys.

3. Katherine wrote a letter.   4. The lions at the zoo are lazy.

5. Naina threw a ball to her dog.

(B) Write a sentence having three nouns in it.

____

(C) Write a sentence having a place and two people in it.

____

Q27](A) <u>Circle the nouns in each sentence:</u>

1. Atulesh ate the apple.   2. Bombay is a big city.

3. I have three pennies and two nickels.   4. Dogs like to chase cats.

5. Bhavna, Vishakha and Devyani sat on the bench.

(B) Write a sentence having a person and an idea in it.

____

(C) Write a sentence using two animals and a place.

____

<u>EXERCISE 16</u>

<u>PLURAL NOUNS</u>

Q28] Circle all the plural nouns.

desks   carpet   chairs   board   teacher   students   pens   pencils
eraser   book   rulers   paper   marker   boxes   headphones   hooks
backpack   tissue   door   posters   music   lesson   blocks
shelf   cat   dogs   man   women   leopard   bus   carpet   girls

pennies   lions   elephant   bunny   giraffe   tigers   gazelle
monkeys   snakes   owl   birds   parrot   bears   trees   foxes
octopus   shark

Q29] Write the plural form for each noun. One is done for you.

1) A dog, many dogs.

2) An eagle, many ___________.

3) A rooster, many __________.

4) A bunny, many ___________.

5) A hamster, many __________.

6) A vulture, many ___________ .

7) A fox, many _________.

8) A chicken, many _________.

9) A horse, many __________.

10) A pony, many ___________.

11) A toy, many ___________.

12) A doll, many __________.

13) A bike, many ___________.

14) A robot, many ___________.

15) A shop, many __________.

16) A clock, many ____________.

17) A train, many ________.

18) A game, many ___________.

19) An ice-cream, many ________.

20) A puzzle, many ___________.

21) A room, many __________.

22) A table, many ___________.

23) A chair, many ___________.

24) A bedsheet, many ____________.

25) A couch, many ___________.

26) A tub, many ____________

27) A closet, many ___________.

28) A door, many __________.

29) A mug, many ___________.

30) A pillow, many ___________.

EXERCISE 17

Singular and plural nouns with matching verbs

Q30] Circle the noun to match the verb.

1)   The girl / girl eats an apple.

2)   The teacher / teachers speaks to the class.
3)   The curtain / curtains are open.
4)   The boot / boots is dirty.
5)   The tea / teas is hot.
6)   The bunny / bunnies eat carrots.
7)   The cheetah / cheetahs runs fast.
8)   The hamster / hamsters are hungry.
9)   The dog / dogs jump in the car.
10) The chick / chicks peck at the grains.
11) The pig / pigs rolls in the mud.
12) The snake / snakes sheds its skin.
13) The spider / spiders has eight legs.
14) The fox / foxes is a cunning animal.
15) My cushion/ cushions are pink.

PROPER & COMMON NOUNS

Q31] Mention which noun are the given words:

1) Enzo ____________   2) car _____________

3) toy ____________   4) Mr. Rai _____________

5) forest ____________   6) California _____________

7) KFC ____________   8) class _____________

9) teacher ____________   10) NIT Park _____________

11) knee ____________   12) Maya _____________

13) carpet ____________   14) bee _____________

15) Metro Police ____________   16) Godavari River _____________

17) Salman ____________   18) school _____________

19) Ms. Kulkarni ____________   20) bus _____________

21) mirror ____________   22) Lily _____________

23) Taj Mahal _______________   24) country _______________

25) door _______________   26) head _______________

27) Amazon _______________   28) train _______________

29) boat _______________   30) The Titanic _______________

EXERCISE 18

CAPITALS AND PROPER NOUNS

Q32] Rewrite the sentences and use a capital for each proper noun.

1) Bhavi pets her cat max.

____

2) mr. goswamy visits the museum in chennai.

____

3) nikhil eats a kashmiri apple.

____

4) misha looks at the qutub minar.

____

5) john goes to delhi public school.

____

6) Jimmy the dog laps the milk.

____

7) ms. rai tells her students about india.

____

8) avighna asks his mom for a snack.

---

9) shanan reads the story of panchatantra to the class.

---

10) smurfs are little blue people.

---

11) india has the best hockey team.

---

12) new york have skyscrapers.

EXERCISE 19

COLLECTIVE NOUNS

Q33] [A] Underline the collective nouns.

1) The hockey team arrived at the rink.   2) Mr. Davuluri's class enjoys science.   3) My friend's family likes camping.   4) I go camping with my Scouts' troop.   5) The group entered the gym together.   6) A school of fish swam by us.   7) The flight of birds was flying south for winter.   8) There was a crowd at the show.   9) The school staff will be away on Friday.   10) How many kittens are in this litter?

[B] Underline the collective nouns.

1) There was a cloud of dust outside the house.   2) Mom gave dad a bunch of flowers.   3) Suchita has a collection of hockey cards. 4) The group of dancers performed well.   5) The class of students listened to the guest speaker.   6) Add it to the stack of books.

7) A posse of fans were following him.   8) A bale of hay is heavy.
9) Her solo was judged by a panel.   10) The cricket team won the game.

Q 34] [A] Fill in the blanks with words from the word bank.

(deck, school, troop, army, collection, gaggle, party, litter, pack, crowd)

1) At the aquarium, we saw a ____________ of fish.

2) An _________ of ants lived behind the shed.

3) Mike has a ____________ of geese on his farm.

4) Mowgli was raised by a ____________ of wolves.

5) The ____________ of people lined up at the doors.

6) The ____________ of kittens is adorable.

7) You shuffle the ____________ of cards first.

8) He has a stamp _______________.

9) The ____________ of friends met for dinner.

10) Suresh goes camping with his Scouts' ____________.

[B] Fill in the blanks with words from the word bank.

(raft, herd, box, bag, class, panel, pod, colony, hive, fleet)

1) There is a ____________ of tissues on the counter.
2) Dad opened a ____________ of chips.
3) We have a ____________ of bees in the yard.
4) There is a ____________ of beavers in the pond.
5) The ____________ of deer entered the forest.
6) The ____________ of students sat at the carpet.
7) The navy has a _________ of ships.
8) They are like peas in a ____________.
9) The ____________ of judges gave the dancer a 10.
10) When swimming on their backs, a _________ of otters is adorable.

EXERCISE 20

NOUNS AS A PERSON PLACE OR THING

Q35] [A] Find the nouns and circle the persons, underline the places and square the things.

1. The actor won an award for his movie about Kashmir.

2. The dog went swimming in the pool.

3. Ice cream and cookies are the best dessert.

4. The pine trees in the forest are taller than most houses.

5. Abhishek wants to take a trip to the beaches.

6. I always wash my face before going to bed.

7. Vivek collects model cars and boats.

8. My brother took a bus to the zoo to see the tigers.

9. My uncle lives in an igloo in Alaska.

10. The team does not practice volleyball in the summer.

[B] Find the nouns and circle the persons, underline the places and square the things.

1. The rides at the county fair were so much fun.

2. Aamir likes to wear a cowboy hat at the rodeo.

3. Rehaan goes to the doctor for a check-up.

4. Our teacher helped us learn about different types of nouns.

5. Riya read a book about Indians from South America.

6. The airplane soared high in the sky above the clouds.

7. The number of clowns in the parade was great.

8. Aunt Nitisha took the kids to the playground.

9. Rutuja had lasagna with Tara for dinner.

10. The rainstorm made the dam overflow with water.

[C] Circle the persons, underline the places and square the things.

post office candle moose grandmother bookshelf basketball airport clock park grape lawyer marsh ice radio Gandhi island uncle forest wheel skateboard pine cone principal whistle tire jump rope monkey butterfly golf cart library bicycle friend backpack notebook country grasshopper eraser cell phone computer carwash firetruck Walt Disney pancake

EXERCISE 21

NOUNS AS DIRECT OBJECTS

Q36] [A] Underline the verbs and circle the direct objects.

1. Madhulee plays the piano.

2. My mom makes the best chocolate cake.

3. The teacher reads a book.

4. The students write their answers.

5. Pratham rides his bike every day.

6. Amisha smells the flowers.

7. Aman and Niranjana finished their meal.

8. The dog chased the squirrel.

9. In the morning, dad makes the bed.

10. The principal drove his car to work.

11. The janitor swept the floor.

12. The boy drank some water.

13. The man reads the paper.

14. Shrushti ate her dessert.

15. Anjali completed her homework.

16. The teacher wrote a sentence.

17. The cat scratches its ear.

18. The dog wagged its tail.

Q37] Underline the verbs and circle the direct objects.

1. The hens laid eggs.   2. Vijaya cleaned her room.   3. Grandma overcooked supper.   4. Vasant answered the phone.   5. The student asked a question.   6. Ashu opened the door.   7. Amrapali dusted the shelf.   8. Suresh climbed the stairs.   9. The children set the table. 10. Aaditi painted the deck.   11. Dad assembled the new structure. 12. Anurag poured juice in the cups.   13. The cleaning person vacuumed the carpet.   14. Everyone awaits his turn.   15. The sisters shared an apple.   16. Mahira drew a heart.   17. Sandhya pulled the curtains.   18. Nitu opened her eyes.   19. Kartikeya prayed to god. 20. Abhishek managed the shop.

EXERCISE 22

COUNTABLE OR UNCOUNTABLE?

Q38] Tell whether the underlined noun is countable or uncountable.

1. _________________ Would you like some <u>milk</u> with your <u>cereal</u>?

2. _________________ will need <u>eggs and salt</u> for this recipe.

3. _________________ Dev asked for more <u>time</u> to finish his test.

4. _________________ Do you have enough <u>information</u> to write your report?

5. _________________ Mani should listen to his coach; he gives good <u>advice</u>.

6. _________________ The teacher wanted his students to put more <u>effort</u> into their assignments.

7. _________________ Listening to good music makes your <u>worries</u> go away.

8. _________________ With enough <u>determination</u>, any task is achievable.

9. _________________ Our living room has so much <u>furniture</u>, there is nowhere to move.

10. _________________ Lara's mom told her to add more <u>flour</u> to the dough before baking the cookies.

11. _________________ She folded the clean towel and put it in the <u>closet</u>.

12. _________________ Mom thinks there is enough <u>time</u> to complete another chore.

13. _________________ Today is laundry day, make sure to bring down all your <u>dirty shirts</u>.

14. _________________ I have one more <u>page</u> to complete for today's homework.

15. _________________ With a little <u>patience</u>, you can finish this puzzle.

16. _________________ I need <u>positivity</u>.

17. _________________ Exercise is an important part of being <u>healthy</u>.

18. _________________ There is so much dust on this <u>bookshelf</u>,we need to clean it.

19. _________________ The <u>snow</u> is so high, it almost reaches the windows.

20. _________________ Would you like me to add some more <u>milk</u> to your hot chocolate?

21. _________________ I would like another plate of <u>pasta</u>, please.

22. _________________ Miranda applied some <u>lotion</u> on her dry hands.

23. _________________ The tub is filled with warm <u>water.</u>

24. _________________ The <u>music</u> is so loud that my ears are ringing.

25. _________________ The <u>sand</u> is nice and warm under my feet.

EXERCISE 23

ABSTRACT NOUNS

Abstract nouns are ideas or concepts - things that you feel or think about.

Q39] [A] Underline the abstract noun(s) in each sentence.

1) We need to think about the importance of friendship.   2) You can see the love this father has for his son.   3) Sam looked at the chocolate cake with greed in his eyes.   4) After thanksgiving dinner everyone patted their stomachs with satisfaction.   5) His eyes were full of hope as he opened his report card.   6) We would like to see justice served.   7) My childhood memories are a source of great joy for me.   8) Would it not be great to have the financial freedom to travel the world?   9) His many years of teaching experience has given him the ability to understand his students.   10) The daughter's acceptance of her mother's advice helped her make her decision. 11) With the right attitude we can remain happy.   12) Hope of success helps us persevere in difficult activities.   13) My grandfather is a man of integrity.   14) It's in her nature to keep silent.   15) Love is not what you say. Love is what you do.   16) Taranjyot has reached a high proficiency in math.   17) The purpose of this worksheet is to help you understand abstract nouns.   18) Are you ready to make the decision now?   19) She reached the zenith of her tennis career at the age of thirty.   20) If we persevere, victory will be ours.

[B] Circle the abstract noun(s) in each sentence.

1) She has a lot of pride.   2) Shrushti is saving her money for her education.   3) You need to have more confidence.   4) Sanjay wants the opportunity to study abroad.   5) You know about the importance of learning English.   6) Happiness means different things to different people.   7) There is a lot of noise coming from that house.   8) The force grandma needed to open the jar was beyond her capacity. 9) You have lost my trust.   10) With a little effort, kindness can become

a habit.   11) Harsh has the ability to do well in the exam.   12) Her courage was admirable for such a young person.   13) I have this great idea for our vacation.   14) The autumn chill is causing some discomfort.   15) It was a pleasure to meet your family.   16) Honesty is the best policy if you want people to trust you.   17) What great luck, we won the lottery.   18) The anticipation was growing as we were getting nearer to Disneyland.   19) You need a sense of humor to work here.   20) Mr. Rai set the standard for competence at work.

EXERCISE 24

CONCRETE AND ABSTRACT

Q40] Write a 'c' for concrete or an 'a' for abstract above the nouns.

1. Gopal saw a movie in October.   2. Sunil put his feet on the table. 3. This melody is wonderful, because it helps with relaxation. 4. You need patience to learn a new skill.   5. After dinner you can have some apple pie.   6. Stress has increased in our city.   7. The loud noise made Sarita upset.   8. The teacher ran away from the mouse. 9. The intelligence of dogs is remarkable.   10. Friendship takes work. You need good friends.   11. Jenna felt love for her hamster.   12. I have hope that all your wishes will come true.   13. Curiosity killed the cat.   14. A dove is a symbol of peace.   15. Your story needs more excitement.   16. Giving gifts spreads joy.   17. The math formula is stored in your memory.   18. I get a lot of satisfaction out of my work.   19. Owning two cars is a luxury in most countries.   20. The child is gaining in maturity.

06

PRONOUNS

Pronoun: A pronoun is a word that takes the place of a noun or group of nouns.

The noun or group of nouns that the pronoun takes the place of is called the **antecedent.**

- The boy said that **he** was tired. In this example, the pronoun **"he"** is referring back to the noun **(antecedent) "boy."**
- Aarya called Ali and invited **him** to go skating with **her.** In this sentence pronouns are "him and her".
- The antecedent of him = Ali and Antecedent of her = Aarya

Aarya called Ali and invited Ali to go skating with Aarya sounds awkward and repetitious.

PRONOUNS AND ITS KINDS:

Sr. no	Types of Pronoun	Definition	Example
1	Personal pronouns	Stand in for specific people or things.	I, you, she, it, we, they, me, him, her, us, them
2	Possessive Pronouns	Indicate ownership or possession.	Mine, yours, his, hers, its, ours, theirs
3	Reflexive Pronouns	Refer back to the subject of the clause	Myself, yourself, himself, herself, itself, ourselves, yourselves, themselves

4	Intensive Pronouns	Used to add emphasis to the subject of the clause (identical in form to reflexive pronouns)	Myself, yourself, himself, herself, itself, ourselves, yourselves, themselves
5	Demonstrative Pronouns	Point of specific things	This, that, these, those
6	Interrogative Pronouns	Used to ask questions	Who, whom, which, what, whose
7	Relative Pronouns	Link clauses or phrases to a noun or pronounce	Who, whom, which, that, whose
8	Indefinite Pronouns	Refer to one or more unspecified people or things	All, another, any, anybody, anyone, anything, each, everybody, everyone, everything, few, many, nobody, none, one, several, some, somebody, someone
9	Reciprocal Pronouns	Refer to a reciprocal relationship	Each other, one another

EXERCISE 25

I or ME

'I' and 'me' are both pronouns, but they are used in different ways. The difference is:

'I' is the subject of the sentence (*"I went to the market."*) and

'me' is the object of the sentence (*"Dad bought me some clothes."*)

Q41] Write I or me on the blank line in each sentence.

1. __________ went to the store with mom.
2. She bought __________ some new clothes.

3. __________ tried them on first.
4. Sakshi made sure they fit __________ well.
5. Rahi helped ________ with the shirt.
6. __________ had trouble with the buttons.
7. After shopping, mom and ________ went to the diner.
8. Shanay ordered a slice of pie for __________.
9. __________ ate it in three bites.
10. She smiled at __________.
11. Avinash and ________ went to football practice.
12. He passed ________ the ball.
13. ________ passed it back.
14. As we played, ______ said: "Pass it to ______. ________ am open!"
15. Adira listened to ______.
16. ______ took the ball and counted one goal.
17. My coach was proud of ______.
18. My friends smiled at __________.
19. The teacher told Marissa and ______ that it was our turn.
20. She and ______ went to the front of the class.
21. ______ placed our poster on the board.
22. Shreya helped ______ with that.
23. Marie started to speak and ______ was listening.
24. She looked at ______ when she was done her part.
25. ______ spoke up and finished the presentation.

<u>EXERCISE 26</u>

Q42] [A]Circle the pronoun in the second sentence and underline the noun it is replacing from the first sentence.

Ex: The teacher is reading a <u>book</u>. It is an interesting one.

1. Take off your boots. They are wet.
2. Call Vaibhav after supper. He seemed worried.

3. Kartik and Divya were playing with the kittens. Then, Divya fed them.
4. Mom and dad went shopping. They bought a new dining set.
5. The farmer brought the cows around. Later, he fixed the fence.
6. Rahul and you are presenting next week. You need to be ready.
7. The woman crossed the street. Then, she entered the store.
8. The children finished their dessert. It was good.
9. His sister put the blankets on the bed. They were soft and warm.
10. The mechanic fixes the car. Then, he puts his tools away.
11. Raj is picking up flowers. They smell so good!
12. Andrew just finished his homework. Now he is reading a book.

[B]

1. Hockey players skate well. They practice everyday.
2. My friend and I are going to the zoo. We are so excited!
3. Be careful with this chair. It has just been repaired.
4. Mr. Verma asked his students to read a new book. They asked what the title was.
5. After school, Hemant and Jenny go to the park. They will play on the swings.
6. Sandhya made some cupcakes. They seem delicious.
7. Julie chose a new book from the library. She opened it to look at the pictures.
8. Alex writes his homework in his notebook. Then, he puts it in his bag.
9. Mom took the milk out of the fridge. She needs it for her recipe.
10. Dad parked the car in the garage. He will wash it later.
11. The firefighter explained his job to the students. Then he took them outside to climb in his fire engine.
12. Disha and Leena are in their new boat, fishing. They bought it last spring.

<u>EXERCISE 27</u>

COMMON PRONOUNS

Pronouns are words that take the place of a noun.

Common pronouns include: I, you, he, she, it, we, they, you, him, her, them, us

Q43] Rewrite each sentence. Change the underlined word(s) to a pronoun.

1. <u>My friends and I</u> are going to the movies.

   ____

2. <u>Tom</u> likes to read books about fairies.

   ____

3. <u>Mom and dad</u> are going out for dinner.

   ____

4. <u>Mrs. Javed</u> gave us homework.

   ____

5. <u>My sock</u> has a hole in it.

   ____

6. <u>The book</u> has a blue cover.

   ____

7. <u>My family</u> likes to go to the zoo.

   ____

8. <u>This chocolate cake</u> is delicious.

   ____

9. <u>Amisha</u> likes to curl up on the sofa and read books.

   ____

10. I drew a picture for <u>my mother</u>.

   ____

11. <u>Cows</u> like to eat grass.

   ____

12. Did <u>dad</u> wash the car?

   ____

13. The pile of clothes on the floor belong to <u>Sushant</u>.

   ____

14. <u>Allen</u> threw the ball for her dog to fetch.

   ____

15. <u>Children</u> are playing in the park.

   ____

16. Do these candies belong to <u>Avi and Mahira</u>?

   ____

17. <u>Sunita</u> likes to write in her journal.

   ____

18. The doll belongs to Kiara.

   ____

19. <u>Disney World</u> is in California.

   ____

20.   The cat ran across the street.

____

21.   Jack plays the ukulele.

____

22.   The apple fell from the tree.

____

EXERCISE 28

REFLEXIVE PRONOUNS

We use a **reflexive pronoun** when we want to **refer back to the subject of the sentence**.

Reflexive pronouns are pronouns that end in -self or -selves.

For example: *I saw myself in the mirror*, they saw *themselves* in the mirror.

Q44] Match the pronouns.

I	itself
He	yourself
She	himself
it	themselves
you	myself
we	yourselves
they	ourselves
you (plural)	herself

IDENTIFY REFLEXIVE PRONOUNS

Q45] [A] Circle the pronoun and draw an arrow to the word it refers to.

1.   Raya folded that big pile of laundry all by himself.

2.   Make sure you buy something for yourself at the mall.
3.   The students were lining themselves in alphabetical order.
4.   As for me, I prefer reading by myself.
5.   The dog was driving itself crazy by chasing its tail.
6.   Can you reach that yourself?
7.   Dad woke himself when he snored.
8.   I cut myself with the scissors.
9.   The girls want to practice by themselves.
10. Your skates won't tie themselves.

[B] Circle the pronoun and draw an arrow to the word it refers to.

1.   The mechanic fixed the car himself.
2.   The children played quietly by themselves.
3.   We looked at new houses ourselves.
4.   Some vacuum cleaners work all by themselves.
5.   The boy himself was scared.
6.   The lights won't turn off by themselves.
7.   I made this soup myself.
8.   Your mom and you are entering yourselves in the dancing contest.
9.   The rose protects itself by closing its petals at night.
10. She made her dress herself.

WRITING REFLEXIVE PRONOUNS

Q46] [A] Fill in the blanks with pronouns ending in "self" or "selves".

1.   I folded my clothes all by _______________.
2.   We treated _______________ to supper at a restaurant.
3.   That cat let _______________ into our house.
4.   Sana and Naayra looked at _______________ in the video.
5.   Nikhil and you walked home by _______________.
6.   Sanjana finished the assignment by _______________.
7.   Give me the form, I will complete it _______________.
8.   Angela played the role by _______________.
9.   Nadia and I cleaned the kitchen by _______________.

10.   You ate this entire cake _____________________!

[B]Fill in the blanks with pronouns ending in "self" or "selves"

1.   Anthony is old enough to walk home by _____________________.
2.   The mole dug this hole by _____________________.
3.   Come on kids, the dishes won't clean _____________________.
4.   You braided your hair by _____________________.
5.   The girls made this cake _____________________.
6.   We see _____________________ in this big window.
7.   You and your friends are building this fort by _____________________.
8.   You can lock the door, I will let _____________________ in.
9.   She ran by _____________________ during the race.
10.   The Rauts are very tall _____________________.

EXERCISE 29

SUBJECT AND OBJECT PRONOUNS

Like the nouns they replace, pronouns can be subjects (*doing something*) or objects (*having something done to it*).

Subject pronouns include I, you, he, she, it, we and they;

object pronouns include me, you him, her, it, us and them.

Q47] [A]Circle the pronoun in each sentence. Write "O" if the pronoun is an object and "S" if the pronoun is a subject.

___S___ 1. They collect sports cards.

_________ 2. Laura called me last night.

_________ 3. We are late again!

_________ 4. The coach will not let us play tonight.

_________ 5. You are going skating this afternoon.

_________ 6. Anita lent you her favorite pencil.

_________ 7. It is time to leave.

_______ 8. There was a math test. Colin found it difficult.

_______ 9. He studied hard for the test.

_______ 10. The teacher gave him the answer.

[B] Circle the pronoun in each sentence. Write "O" if the pronoun is an object and "S" if the pronoun is a subject.

_______ 1. Are you done with the salt? Put it there.

_______ 2. It is raining again today.

_______ 3. We are the best at soccer.

_______ 4. The mailman gave us our parcel.

_______ 5. You will find the story interesting.

_______ 6. My friend saw you at the mall.

_______ 7. I have time to help with the dishes.

_______ 8. My mom made me a key for the house.

_______ 9. She prefers lemonade to orange juice.

_______ 10. The principal asked him a question.

PRONOUN AGREEMENT

Pronouns must **agree in number and gender** with the nouns they replace.

Q48] Select the correct pronoun from the word bank.

[A] [he   it   their   they   she   mine   they   both]

1. Manoj and Dolly said _______ have to go to school on Friday.
2. Bipin thought that __________ could stay up until midnight.
3. That is not your car. It's __________.
4. The dog was sick, and __________ wouldn't play fetch with me.
5. Juliet was going to the store when __________ fell off of her bike.
6. John and James asked __________ parents if they could have some money.

[B] [any   **it**   **no**   **one**   **they**   **she**   **mine**   **both**]

7. _____________ has to do homework this weekend.
8. _____________ could talk to her friends on the phone on Tuesdays.
9. _____________ boys thought their parents were going to buy them new shoes.
10. The cat was happy, and _____________ purred loudly.
11. _____________ both wanted to go to Mexico for vacation.
12. _____________ student would be glad to have a day off to play in the snow.

[C] [**it**   **she**   **his**   **mine**   **they**   **he**   **its**]

13. Daniel thought that ___ was going to win the race.
14. Robert lost because _____________ shoe fell off on his way.
15. That is not your cat. It's _____________.
16. The dog licked _____________ bowl and took a nap.
17. Lara said _____________ was going to be at the concert tomorrow.
18. James and Aaron asked if _____________ could have pizza for breakfast.

[D] [**no**   **one**   **any**   **both**   **they**   **she it**   **theirs**]

19. Is that your parents' car? Yes, it is _____________.
20. _____________ ate all of her soup at lunch.
21. _____________ teachers are getting new classrooms.
22. _____________ likes to wake up early to go to school.
23. _____________ dog would love to eat a steak every day.
24. _____________ want to play soccer in the park.

EXERCISE 30

WHO, WHOM or WHOSE

Who is the subject of the sentence, the person completing an action.

Whom is the object or receiver of that action.

Whose refers to possession.

Q49][A] Fill in the blank with who, whom, or whose.

1. Do you know _______ is coming to the party?
2. The student to _____________ I spoke was very kind.
3. You are eating dinner with _____________?
4. I have no idea _____________ notebook this is.
5. I saw a man _____________ was at least seven feet tall.
6. _____________ is your favorite teacher?
7. She doesn't know _____________ book was left behind.
8. My mom asked _____________ made the card for her.
9. For _____________ did you make this birthday cake?
10. _____________ car is parked in our garage?

[B] Fill in the blank with who, whom, or whose.

1. The girl with _______ I worked was very quiet.
2. You are talking to _____________?
3. Does anyone know _____________ backpack this is?
4. She talked to a woman _____________ knows my mom.
5. _____________ was at the park today?
6. Stefan has no clue _____________ sock was in his car.
7. My dad wondered _____________ forgot to lock the door.
8. With _____________ did you ride to school today?
9. _____________ cat is walking in our yard?
10. Mrs. Smith asked _____________ had finished the assignment.

[C] Fill in the blank with who, whom, or whose.

1. With whom are you travelling to Chicago?
2. Did you find out ______________ house we are visiting?
3. The man ______________ came with us is my uncle.
4. ______________ is that girl with your cousin?
5. Sharon doesn't know ______________ pencil was on the desk.
6. We asked ______________ was making dinner tonight.
7. For ______________ did you buy that gift?
8. ______________ baby is crying all night?
9. My brother wondered ______________ took his backpack.
10. Did you see the boy ______________ bike was stolen?

EXERCISE 31

RELATIVE PRONOUN: THAT or WHICH

'*That*' is used to define information essential to the meaning of the sentence.

'*Which*' provides non-essential information.

Q50] [A] Fill in the blank with that or which.

1. The hand <u>that</u> hurts the most is my left hand.
2. When he saw the house, ______________ had six huge windows, he started to cry.
3. I like to buy cheeses ______________ taste delicious.
4. Did you see the dog ______________ has three legs?
5. I wore the dress ______________ my mom bought me.
6. The party, ______________ was yesterday, was a big success.
7. Robert won the prize, ______________ was exciting for his family.
8. The table ______________ is broken needs to get repaired soon.
9. The test, ______________ was a surprise to everyone, did not go well.
10. We saw a turtle ______________ looked just like my old turtle, Speedy.

[B] Fill in the blank with that or which.

1. My favorite movie, _________ is very popular, is about a girl in India.
2. You ate the pizza _____________ I love for breakfast.
3. The book _____________ I read was fantastic.
4. My teacher assigned a book, _____________ had 100 pages, for homework during break.
5. We saw the lake _____________ had beautiful blue waters on our way to my house.
6. The car _____________ stopped in front of us belongs to my sister.
7. My birthday, _____________ is February 14, is always my favorite day of the year.
8. The computer _____________ I got as a gift has worked for ten years.
9. We bought a calendar _____________ has flowers on the cover.
10. The new house, _____________ is located on Patel Street, has a purple door.

[C] Fill in the blank with that or which.

1. Who is _________ kid on the swing?
2. We saw the calf _____________ loves to eat the grass in our yard.
3. The shop, _____________ opens at noon, serves kachoris on Wednesdays.
4. My car, _____________ is in the garage, needs to be repaired before our tour.
5. Did you see the project _____________ was left on the table?
6. My homework, _________ was assigned yesterday, is due tomorrow.
7. My favorite song, _____________ is very popular, plays on the Spotify all the time.
8. Did you see _________ lizard on the wall?
9. The door, _____________ was open all night, let in a breeze.
10. The new phone, _____________ is now available in stores, takes amazing photos.

EXERCISE 32

POSSESSIVE, RELATIVE & INDEFINITE PRONOUNS

A possessive pronoun refers to a specific owner: mine, yours, my, hers, his, its, your, etc.

Q51] Fill in the blanks with the correct possessive pronouns from the word banks.

Possessive pronouns: its, mine, their, her, ours, your, hers, yours, his, theirs

1. The dog was busy eating _____ bone.
2. The little girl couldn't find _______ favorite baby doll.
3. My parents love to visit _______ friends who live in Mexico.
4. These cookies? They are all _______.
5. We were hoping that the shiny, red sports car was going to be _______
6. She grabbed the plate of food because she thought it was _______.
7. Is this _______ house?
8. The cat loved sleeping on _______ blanket.
9. The boy was looking for ___ parents.
10. Did you go to _______ house after school?
11. I bought a giant candy bar because I wanted it to be all _______.
12. That suitcase isn't yours; it is definitely _______.

Q52] Fill in the blanks with the correct Relative pronouns from the word banks:

A relative pronoun connects a phrase to a noun/ pronoun: who, which, that, whom, etc.

[who, which, that, whoever, whichever]

1. _______ went to Rajasthan will give the report on Jaipur.
2. I saw the lady _______ lives in the house alone.
3. These little dogs ate the bones _______ were thrown on the street.
4. I didn't know _______ resort to choose.

5. _______ is wearing the blue shirt in the picture looks very happy.
6. My doctor works in the building _______ is on the corner.
7. _______ choice you make will be a good one.
8. Do you know the girl _______ goes to the music class?
9. _______ lives in this house needs to mow the grass.
10. I don't know _______ restaurant is the most delicious.
11. The teacher _______ teaches mathematics loves to solve problems.
12. The boy prefers a seat _______ is close to the front of the room.

Q53] Fill in the blanks with the correct Indefinite pronouns from the word banks:

An indefinite pronoun doesn't refer to anything specific: all, any, each, some, several, etc.

[all, any, someone, anything, nobody each, some, several]

1. _______ like adventure.
2. _______ of my family members live in Coimbatore.
3. She saw _______ who looked just liked her mom.
4. I was wondering if you had _______ ideas for the new store.
5. I cannot believe I ate _______ of the snacks.
6. _______ student needs to bring one box of tissues to donate.
7. Did you find _______ of the answers to the homework?
8. I was only able to find ____ of them.
9. _______ of my teachers have decided to go take a class this weekend.
10. _______ person can start a business in my town.
11. I was looking for _______ who would like to go to the park with me.
12. Is there _______ special you'd like to do for your birthday?

EXERCISE 33

Q54] Fill in the blanks with the correct pronouns.

(i) Peter and I are brothers. _____________ share a bedroom together.
(ii) Saina isn't well. Dad is taking _______ to see a doctor.

(iii)   My brother is a teacher. _______ teaches English. All of ______ students like ________ very much.

(iv)   Children, are making too much noise! Ask ________ to stay quiet.

(v)   Who are those people? Where are _________ from?

(vi)   Mom is a doctor. _______ works in a hospital.

(vii)   The sky is getting dark. _____ is going to rain.

(viii)   John, we are all waiting for ______. Are you coming with ____?

(ix)   May ____ borrow your pen? Yes, of course. When can you return ____ to _____ ?

(x)   What are _______ reading, Jennifer?

Q55] Fill suitable pronoun in the following.

(i)   _______ and I are old friends.

(ii)   _______ rained very heavily last night.

(iii)   ________ must not boast of riches.

(iv)   ________ fought and got hurt.

(v)   Uneasy lies _______ head wears a crown.

(vi)   _______ is done cannot be undone.

(vii)   All the four members of the family quarrelled with ________.

(viii)   ________ of them were soldiers.

(ix)   Recite what _______ have learnt.

(x)   Do good to those ________ hate you.

EXERCISE 34

Q56] Choose the correct word:

(i)   I shall do it (myself, himself)

(ii)   My book is better than (mine, her, yours)

(iii)   She told (herself, me) a story.

(iv)   Who is there? It is (I, me).

(v)   Mind it. It is between you and (I, me).

(vi)   (whose, which) picture do you prefer?

(vii)   (either, each) of you can do it.

(viii)   (whatever, whichever) you do, do it well.
(ix)   Don't leave it (what, whatever) happens.
(x)   Your brother (who, whom) everybody likes is very expert.

Q57] Fill in suitable pronoun in the following.

(i)   _________ are these boys?
(ii)   _________ car broke down?
(iii)   _________ caused the explosion?
(iv)   _________ did you go with?
(v)   _________ of these do you like?
(vi)   Trees drop _________ leaves in autumn.
(vii)   He can't share _________
(viii)   I did it _________
(ix)   The noise _________ he made woke everybody up.
(x)   The story is of a man _________ wife betrays him.

Q58] Replace the underlined words with the appropriate pronouns in the box. Use capital letters when necessary.

[she   her   he   him   it   we   us   they   them   him]

(i)   I called Mr. Benjamin this morning and gave <u>Mr. Benjamin</u> my homework.
(ii)   Veer likes computer games but <u>Veer</u> doesn't play <u>computer games</u> very often.
(iii)   Neil Armstrong was born in 1930. <u>Neil Armstrong</u> landed on the moon in 1969.
(iv)   Penguins don't live near the North Pole. <u>Penguins</u> live near the South Pole.
(v)   My aunt lives in Toronto but <u>my aunt</u> often comes to visit my family and me.
(vi)   If you have your ticket, you can give <u>your ticket</u> to that man over there.
(vii)   First, my friend and I went shopping. Later, <u>my friend and I</u> went home.

(viii)   Where was Sarah? I didn't see <u>Sarah</u> at the party last week.

(ix)   Johnson is a really nice guy. I like <u>Johnson</u> a lot.

(x)   The planet Mars has two moons. The <u>two moons</u> are both very small.

(xi)   I really liked the cake. Unfortunately, I didn't have time to finish the <u>cake</u>.

(xii)   Shiva and I paid for the meal but the waiter forgot to bring <u>Shiva and me</u> the food.

EXERCISE 35

Q59] Replace the underlined word/words in each sentence with correct pronoun.

1.   Rajesh is five feet tall. Anu is only four and a half feet tall. <u>Rajesh</u> is taller than <u>Anu</u>.

2.   Deepak saw Nitin. <u>Deepak</u> called <u>Nitin</u>. Then <u>Deepak and Nitin</u> walked together.

3.   Jatin and his sister thought one of the gold fish was hungry, so <u>Jatin and his sister</u> fed the gold fish.

4.   I met Amit and Esha. I had not seen <u>Amit and Esha</u> for a long time. I asked <u>Amit</u> if <u>Amit</u> was still single.

5.   Deer have antlers. <u>Deer</u> must be very proud of <u>their antlers</u>.

Q60] Use the relative pronoun 'who' to join these sentences. The first one has been done for you.

1. The drunken man was arrested by the police. The drunken man punched me repeatedly.

____

2. The man apologised to me. He stepped on my toes.

____

3. She did most of the talking. She was the hostess.

____

4. The fishermen were hailed as heroes. They caught a shark.

____

5. The hunter was short-sighted. He saw a cheetah and thought it was a leopard.

____

EXERCISE 36

Q61] Correct the following sentences:

   (i)   Which are you playing with?
   (ii)   Where do you want to see?
   (iii)   Whose did you talk to?
   (iv)   What book did you borrow, this or that.
   (v)   Which is wrong with you.
   (vi)   Who did you like to drink?
   (vii)   What is your dress maker?
   (viii)   Who skirt are you wearing?
   (ix)   Who makes tea sweet?
   (x)   Who did you talk?

(xi)   What is she looking?
(xii)   What do you take care?
(xiii) Whom was he running?
(xiv)   What do you work?
(xv)   What do you want to sit?
(xvi)   What book is yours, this or that?
(xvii) What do you want to play?
(xviii) He gave his book his wife.
(xix)   What is your carpenter?
(xx)   Who do you find in this picture?

07

ADJECTIVES

An *adjective* is a word that modifies a noun or a pronoun. In general, adjectives usually give us more information about a noun or pronoun by describing it or providing more information about it. It is a part of speech used in a sentence **to define the qualities of a noun.**

There are mainly 12 types of adjectives, they are as follows:

1] **Possessive adjective**: It expresses possession. They modify a noun by telling whom it belongs to. It also answers the question "whose".

Ex: his, her, its, my, our, your, their.

2] **Absolute adjective**: This adjective doesn't have any comparative or superlative degree.

Ex: perfect, final, total, unique, equal, etc.

3] **Adjective of Quality:** Adjective showing the kind of quality of nouns or pronouns is called adjective of quality.

Ex: cold, rich, wise, smart, brave, honest, etc.

4] **Adjective of quantity**: The adjectives which show the quantity of a noun are called adjectives of quantity.

Ex: much, enough, half, little, etc.

5] **Adjective of number:** Numeral adjectives are those that express numbers of the noun or pronoun. It also shows how many persons or things are meant.

Ex: three, four, sixth, ten, each, etc.

6] **Adjective of shape:** The adjective which represent the shape of pronoun is called an adjective of shape.

Ex: circle, triangular, pentagon, rectangular, etc.

7] **Adjective of color:** They show color of noun or pronoun.

Ex: yellow, green, red, violet, etc.

8] **Adjectives of origin:** Adjectives which describe another person or thing in origin.

Ex: Indian, Hindu, American, Christian, Italian, Muslim, etc.

9] **Demonstrative adjectives:** They show that which and what thing is meant.

Ex: this, that, these, those

10] **Interrogative Adjective:** Are used with nouns to ask questions.

Ex: Which car?, Whose book?, What time?

11] **Distributive adjective:** They refer to each one of a number.

Ex: Each, everyone, etc.

12] **Indefinite adjective:** These adjectives point out the nouns. They often tell "how many" or "how much" of something.

Ex: All, any, another, both, etc.

EXERCISE 37

Q62] Circle the adjectives.

Pretty girl boy tall hair fat shirt car chair grey cat door short dog expensive lamp delicious pie final card soft rock old clothes young thin happy rough dirty clean Polite child teacher generous person flat table round

cushion shiny sofa brilliant method important lesson tasty
recipe stairs sweet dessert sour sticky handle hot coffee
cold water warm soup wood icy kind move little picture
green logs skinny deep clear toy cook slow zebra ride
game wide loud run table mail round beetle sister plane
speedy cold

Q63] (A) Circle the adjectives.

curly photo hollow reading jolly bench brown walk fast
angry cross card fancy flat horse

(B) Complete the sentences using the adjectives from above.

1. Anwarya's hair is long and __________. 2. The tree stump is
__________. 3. My mom wore a __________ dress. 4. Chocolate
bars are __________. 5. The __________ man smiled all the time.
6. A pancake is __________.

Q64] (A) Circle the adjectives.

Fuzzy bear book sister skip race blue plain sorry dark
kind little cat rainy bush

(B) Complete the sentences using the adjectives from above.

1. My blanket is warm and __________. 2. The sky is __________
and sunny. 3. The __________ day helped the flowers grow.
4. I sleep better in a __________ room. 5. My __________ aunt gave me
a dollar. 6. She wore a red shirt and a __________ skirt.

Q65] Use an adjective to complete the sentence.

1) Meera has a ______ bird.
2) Your hair is ________.
3) My dad is wearing a ________ sweater.
4) The ______ car is parked beside ours.
5) This ______ blanket is mine.

6)   I would like the _______ pen.
7)   The _____________ pie was made by mom.
8)   I find this homework _______________.
9)   Mary has a __________ friend named Sameer.
10)   Your friend Leena is ____________.

EXERCISE 38

Q66] (A) Add an adjective to each sentence.

1)   Bhavya has a __________________ bicycle.
2)   There are two _____________ pillows on the couch.
3)   The ____________ girl stands at the end of the line.
4)   The ___________ man helped the lady cross the street.
5)   Mrs. Reddy is a __________ teacher.
6)   The _____________ light hurts my eyes.
7)   Your ___________ shoes left marks all over the floor.
8)   This __________ book is still interesting.
9)   Cynthia has _____________ eyes.
10)   Nancy wears a __________ dress to the dinner.

(B) Add an adjective to each sentence.

1)   The ____________ students lined up in silence.
2)   The __________ sun warmed the children in the yard.
3)   Nick and Priya swam in a __________ lake.
4)   Dad caught a __________ fish this morning.
5)   Mom does not like a ___________ bedroom.
6)   There is nothing like a ____________ meal at the end of the day.
7)   Put your _________ dishes in the sink.
8)   Leave your ________ coat on the hook by the door.
9)   Will you introduce your __________ friend to your class?
10)   The ____________ boy went to sleep.

EXERCISE 39

ADJECTIVES AFTER NOUNS

Q67] (A) In each sentence, circle the adjective and underline the noun it describes.

1) The monster was scary.
2) The building is high.
3) The book was thick.
4) My watch is green.
5) The man seemed unhappy.
6) Our holiday is long.
7) The dog was stinky!
8) The ice was slippery.
9) The teacher was nice.
10) The music was loud.

(B) In each sentence, circle the adjective and underline the noun it describes.

1) The children were happy to go inside.
2) I read the red book.
3) The elephants are big.
4) They live in a grand house.
5) The fresh flowers were in a vase.
6) The race is ten kilometers long.
7) The flowers smelled good.
8) You wrote a wonderful story.
9) Nina is restless.
10) Rumi is clumsy.

EXERCISE 40

Q68] Add an adjective to each sentence.

1. Misha walked her dog. ____
2. Freddy took his sister to the park. _______________________________________
3. The teacher reads a story. ____
4. Mom made fish for dinner. ____
5. My friend lost his parrot. ____
6. The player scored a goal. ____
7. My dad made a tree house. ____

8. Bilo is a dog. _______________________________________

9. The girls were playing with their toys._______________________

10. Manasi wears a coat. _______________________________

11. Nitin finished his exercise. ___________________________

12. The friends built a fort together._______________________

13. The girl curled her hair. ____________________________

14. Tom is writing a story. _____________________________

15. The wind picked up the leaves._______________________

16. The man walked to the house._______________________

17. The grass needs to be cut. ___________________________

Degrees of Adjectives

Positive	Comparative	Superlative
Beautiful	more beautiful than	the most beautiful
Big	bigger than	the biggest
black	blacker than	the blackest
bright	brighter than	the brightest
clean	cleaner than	the cleanest
clever	cleverer than	the cleverest
confused	more confused than	the most confused
difficult	more difficult than	the most difficult
dirty	dirtier than	the dirtiest
fascinating	more fascinating than	the most fascinating
famous	more famous than	the most famous

far	farther / further than	the farthest/ furthest
fast	faster than	the fastest
fat	fatter than	the fattest
fierce	fiercer than	the fiercest
late	later than	the latest
old	older than	the oldest
poor	poorer than	the poorest
proud	prouder than	the proudest
quiet	quieter than	the quietest
sharp	sharper than	the sharpest
short	shorter than	the shortest
slow	slower than	the slowest
small	smaller than	the smallest
strange	stranger than	the strangest
strong	stronger than	the strongest
tall	taller than	the tallest
thin	thinner than	the thinnest
ugly	uglier than	the ugliest
weak	weaker than	the weakest
wise	wiser than	the wisest
young	younger than	the youngest

EXERCISE 41

COMPARING ADJECTIVES

"Most" compares three or more things. "More" compares two things.

Q 69] Put more or most in front of each adjective.

1. Football is ____________ dangerous than golf.
2. Spaghetti is the ____________ wonderful meal there is.
3. You ask the ____________ interesting questions.
4. Urvashi is ____________ delicate than her sister Sita.
5. The couch is ____________ comfortable than the chair.
6. This ceremony is the ____________ elegant that I have ever seen.
7. Cats are the ____________ interesting pets.
8. Science is ____________ difficult than arts.
9. Honey is ____________ natural than refined sugar.
10. Panda bears are the ____________ loveable animals.

Q 70] Write "er" or "est" after each adjective.

With short adjectives (tall, soft), we can add "er" or "est" to compare things in a sentence.

"er" compares 2 things, "est" compares 3 or more things

1. Max is the cute______ dog on the street.
2. Priya is loud______ than Maria in the classroom.
3. I wear my hair short______ than you.
4. Your chair is the hard______ here.
5. Mom has the soft______ hands.
6. Dad's pants are large____ than mine.
7. This is the big______ bowl of popcorn I have ever seen!
8. Cats are quiet______ than dogs.
9. Snow White was the fair______ of them all.
10. You arrived late______ than Alex.

Q71] Choose the right words to complete each sentence.

Hint: Add more before long adjectives; Add "er" after short adjectives.

1.   Selena was the ________________ girl in the room.
     (happier / happiest)

2.   Raya is ________________ than Max in class.
     (more focused / most focused)

3.   The mouse is ________________ than the cat and got away.
     (faster / fastest)

4.   Cutting wood is the ________________ activity I have ever
     done. (more demanding / most demanding)

5.   The CN tower is the ________________ one in Canada.
     (taller / tallest)

6.   My bed is ________________ than my parent's bed.
     (more comfortable / most comfortable)

7.   The sun is ________________ than the moon.
     (brighter / brightest)

8.   The ________________ sports are called extreme sports.
     (more dangerous / most dangerous)

9.   This is the ________________ test I have completed.
     (harder / hardest)

10. Water from the fridge is ________________ than from the tap.
     (colder / coldest)

EXERCISE 42

FINDING ADJECTIVES IN TEXTS

Q72] Circle the adjectives in the story.

During Pioneers times, life was not easy. The men worked hard at removing the tall trees from their land to build their small log homes. They labored from dawn until dusk to build a solid home for their families. The women also worked hard. They planted vegetable gardens and tended to them all summer long to make sure they would have fresh food to put on the table. They washed dirty clothes by hand using square soap they made from scratch. The many children helped a lot with the easier chores. They milked the cows and collected the eggs from the chicken coop. They cleaned the filthy stable and fed the hungry animals. They completed all their daily chores before walking to school. Life as a pioneer was hard, and people worked for every bit of food they ate.

Q73] Circle the adjectives in the story.

Nathan's family went to the beach last summer. His mother packed their big suitcases with several bathing suits, large beach towels as well as many summer outfits. They placed the blue suitcases in the back of their vehicle and took their places. Nathan's dad drove from their house to the nice cottage they rented on the beach. They parked the car and brought their bags into the cottage. Nathan picked a cozy room with bunkbeds. His sister chose the pink room. Their parents took the largest room. There was a tiny kitchen in the cottage and an equally small living room. Soon, they were ready for their first afternoon at the beach. Carrying their light beach bags, wearing flip flops, they walked on the sandy beach near the sea. The kids played in the gentle waves while their parents looked at them from the beach. They had a wonderful time and plan to return next summer.

Q74] Circle the adjectives in the story.

These are the steps to make a delicious sandwich. First, you need two slices of fresh bread. Then, using a dull knife, spread mustard on the bread. Select your favorite cold meat. Mine is black forest ham. Pick two slices of the thin meat and place it on top of the bread. You can add a slice of swiss cheese to the meat. Get some lettuce and pull a few leaves. Add them to the pile. Put the second slice on top to close your sandwich and cut it with a sharp knife. Place your sandwich on a clean plate and sit down at the table. Your delicious sandwich is ready to eat. Enjoy!

EXERCISE 43

Q75] Is the underlined word a normal adjective ("N"), comparative ("C") or superlative ("S")?

___________ 1. Mary is the <u>wisest</u> girl I know.

___________ 2. Karan is <u>tall</u> for his age.

___________ 3. James is <u>lazier</u> than Robert.

___________ 4. Peanuts are <u>cheaper</u> than cashews.

___________ 5. The closet is the <u>fullest</u> it's ever been.

___________ 6. This pillow is <u>lighter</u> than the other.

___________ 7. Phil played the <u>longest.</u>

___________ 8. Anita's flowers are <u>smaller</u> than Mary's.

___________ 9. The suitcase is <u>heavy</u>.

___________ 10. Your hair is <u>shorter</u> than before.

___________ 11. This is your <u>bluest</u> dress.

___________ 12. I prefer his <u>earlier</u> songs.

___________ 13. He is getting <u>redder</u> by the second.

___________ 14. Wear a <u>clean</u> shirt.

EXERCISE 44

FEWER AND LESS

Q76] Complete the sentences with either 'fewer' or 'less'.

Use 'fewer' for objects that can be counted. Ex: 5 eggs

Use 'less' with nouns that are not countable. Ex: rice

1. Mayuri has _______cards than Kirti.
2. Grandpa has ___________ time to play than me.
3. This recipe takes ___________ flour than the other.
4. I will have ___________ breads for breakfast than you.
5. You should have ___________ difficulty with this homework.
6. This page has ___________ physics problems to complete.
7. ___________ people came to the Royal fair this year.
8. The crowd was ___________ animated than last year.
9. Janhavi lost ___________ teeth than you.
10. The admission costs ___________ money than last time.
11. In winter, there are ___________ choices of games to play at recess.
12. Thankfully, they are making ___________ noise than before.

GOOD AND BETTER

Q77] Complete the sentences with either 'good' or 'better'.

Use 'good' to describe one thing. Ex: You have a good cell phone.

Use 'better' to compare two things. Ex: Lara has a better bracelet than Kajal.

1. The choco pie is so_______.
2. The cake is ___________ than the pudding.
3. With all this rain, it is a ___________ thing you came in when you did.

4.   Your loafers are still ___________, you do not need new ones.

5.   The green marker is ___________ than the black one.

6.   There are ___________ ways to solve the problem than the one he picked.

7.   Rashmi told a ___________ story than you.

8.   Nishant is ___________ at playing the drums.

9.   This seems like a ___________ idea.

10.   This beat is ___________ than the one you played earlier.

11.   There is no ___________ sitter than Sushmita.

12.   You picked a ___________ strategy to win the game.

MORE AND MANY

Q78] Complete the sentences with either 'more' or 'many'.

Use 'many' for items which can be counted. Ex: 3 oranges

Use 'more' with nouns which cannot be counted. Ex: oil

1.   There were___________ questions on the quiz.

2.   The quiz takes ___________ time to complete when you are careful.

3.   Tina sold ___________ lemonade than Sagar.

4.   ___________ students were confused by the chemistry problem.

5.   There were ___________ players at the polo practice.

6.   ___________ effort went into this book project.

7.   The train had so ___________ cars, we did not know which one was ours.

8.   You will need to clear ___________ space if you want to fit study table in your room.

9.   I need ___________ light to see what I am doing.

10.   It takes ___________ tries before you can get it right.

11.   Do you want some ___________ money?

12.   There were ___________ people in line ahead of us.

ADJECTIVES WITH "-ER" AND "-EST"

Q79] Choose the correct adjective.

To compare two things, add –er. Ex: Reynolds is cheaper than the Parker pen.

To compare three or more things, add –est. Ex: Montex is the cheapest pen.

1. Akshita is the_________ girl in her class. (tall, taller, tallest)
2. Nathan is ___________ than Suraj. (short, shorter, shortest)
3. Your dog is the ___________ amongst all. (fast, faster, fastest)
4. The kittens are even ________ than their mother (cute, cuter, cutest)
5. This is the ___________ race I have ever participated in. (long, longer, longest)
6. My farm house is ___________ than yours. (big, bigger, biggest)
7. Your friend is the ___________ girl in the pageant. (pretty, prettier, prettiest)
8. Abhishek is the ___________ boy in the house. (happy, happier, happiest)
9. You are the ___________ player I know. (fair, fairer, fairest)
10. Your cat is ___________ than mine. (cuddly, cuddlier, cuddliest)
11. Tina's bedroom is ___________ than Alexa. (neat, neater, neatest)
12. These oranges are the ___________ I have ever tasted. (juicy, juicier, juiciest)
13. My brother Alaric is the _________person in the house. (lazy, lazier, laziest)
14. Victoria is ___________ than Elizabeth. (smart, smarter, smartest)
15. Apples are ___________ than oranges at the store. (cheap, cheaper, cheapest)
16. Our principal is the ___________ man there is. (kind, kinder, kindest)
17. Jonathan is ___________ than Freddy. (bold, bolder, boldest)
18. Jeremy is the ___________ student of the class. (young, younger, youngest)

19. My dad is ___________ than yours. (old, older, oldest)
20. These are the ___________ clothes I have ever owned. (cool, cooler, coolest)
21. These fruits are the ___________ in the store. (fresh, fresher, freshest)
22. Noah will arrive ___________ than he thought. (late, later, latest)
23. This training is ___________ than the one we had last week. (tough, tougher, toughest)
24. This rope is ___________ than that one. (long, longer, longest)
25. This light is much ___________ than that one. (bright, brighter, brightest)
26. Jim is the ___________ dog I know. (hungry, hungrier, hungriest)
27. The police officer looks ___________ than the thief he arrested. (angry, angrier, angriest)
28. Whales are the ___________ mammals on earth. (large, larger, largest)
29. This skirt is ___________ than the one I wore yesterday. (new, newer, newest)
30. The scared kid looked ___________ now that his mother arrived. (calm, calmer, calmest)

EXERCISE 45

Order of Adjectives:

quantity / number, quality / opinion, size, age, shape, color, origin, material, purpose

Q80] Choose the correct order of adjectives. Write the letter on the line. One is done for you.

__A__ 1. A. five, little, kids B. little, five, kids.

______ 2. A. a handsome, young, man B. a young, handsome, man

______ 3. A. full, three, boxes B. three, full, boxes

_______ 4. A. Japanese, large, cars B. large, Japanese, cars

_______ 5. A. four, round, red, tables B. four, red, round, tables

_______ 6. A. Chinese, delicious, food B. delicious, Chinese, food

_______ 7. A. a smelly, old, kitchen, towel B. an old, kitchen, smelly, towel

_______ 8. A. a cool, new, red, sports, car B. a new, red, cool, sports, car

_______ 9. A. two, little, ugly, pillows B. two, ugly, little, pillows

_______ 10. A. a beautiful, Jamaican, sunrise B. a Jamaican, beautiful, sunrise

_______ 11. A. a pretty, purple, skirt B. a purple, pretty, skirt

_______ 12. A. eighteen, soda, large, bottles B. eighteen, large, soda, bottles

_______ 13. A. three, blue, square, tiles B. three, square, blue, tiles

_______ 14. A. a beautiful, big, silver, truck B. a silver, big, beautiful, truck

_______ 15. A. seven, old, checkered table cloths B. seven, checkered, old, table, cloths

_______ 16. A. an American, fuzzy, rabbit B. a fuzzy, America, rabbit

_______ 17. A. two, pretty, sparkly, blue B. two, blue, pretty, sparkly, dresses

_______ 18. A. a lazy, young, man B. a young, lazy, man

_______ 19. A. five, shiny, gold, rings B. five, gold, shiny, rings

_______ 20. A. four, ancient, large, statues B. four, large, ancient statues

_______ 21. A. a new, Irish song B. an Irish, new song

_______ 22. A. a young, talented actress B. a talented, young actress

_______ 23. A. a blue, round, gem B. a round, blue, gem

_______ 24. A. a strange, little, yellow, leaf B. a little, strange, yellow, leaf

______ 25. A. a funny, old, actor B. an old, funny, actor

______ 26. A. a long, Russian, tale B. a Russian, long, tale

______ 27. A. three, pink, little, pigs B. three, little, pink, pigs

______ 28. A. a large, white, moving truck B. a white, large, moving truck

______ 29. A. five, yellow, bright, stars B. five, bright, yellow, stars

______ 30. A. a small, strong, American, woman B. a strong, American, small, woman

EXERCISE 46

Q81] [A] Make negative adjectives from the given words by adding prefix to it. Use Un- ,in- , im- , ir- ,dis-

Sensitive______________Polite______________Responsible______________

Possible______________Logical______________Obedient______________

Pleasant______________Legal______________Honest______________

Fair______________

[B] Add adjectives:

1. The boys eat.......... than girls.
2. A group of individuals is............. than a single individual
3. She is the .... cunning lady of the whole group
4. It is always good to work for a...........
5. Milk is...........
6. This road is the............ one in the town.
7. Black is the.........
8. Birbal was a............. man.
9. I can run........... than she.
10. This is the........ gift I have ever received.

Q82] Fill in the blanks with the correct form of degree of the adjectives given in brackets.

1. Nadira was the most............ girl that Salim had ever seen. (beautiful)
2. I have not seen any child that is .... than Sharvari. (naughty)
3. To preach is........ than to practise. (easy)
4. These lights are....... than those ones, (bright)
5. Hollywood movies are great but not as.............as Bollywood movies. (interesting)
6. Mumbai is much............ than any other city in Maharashtra. (busy)
7. Who is the........... actress according to you? (pretty)
8. I think, this cloth is................... that we purchased earlier.(fine)
9. Autumn is the .... season that I have ever loved. (lovely)
10. Living in Bangalore is .... than living in Hyderabad. (expensive)

Basic Adjectives List:

1. abrupt	2. acidic	3. adorable	4. amiable	5. amused
6. juicy	7. appetizing	8. average	9. kind	10. blushing
11. bored	12. brave	13. bright	14. broad	15. bulky
16. burly	17. charming	18. scary	19. cheerful	20. chubby
21. clean	22. clear	23. cloudy	24. clueless	25. clumsy
26. creepy	27. crooked	28. cruel	29. tender	30. curved
31. terrible	32. dangerous	33. dashing	34. decayed	35. deceitful
36. deep	37. defeated	38. shallow	39. delicious	40. disturbed
41. dizzy	42. selfish	43. drained	44. dull	45. eager
46. ecstatic	47. thick	48. elegant	49. silky	50. embarrassed
51. enchanting	52. energetic	53. enormous	54. extensive	55. exuberant

56. fancy	57. fantastic	58. fierce	59. naughty	60. flat
61. salty	62. precious	63. foolish	64. nervous	65. fresh
66. friendly	67. frightened	68. pleasant	69. funny	70. fuzzy
71. proud	72. gentle	73. ghastly	74. giddy	75. gigantic
76. glamorous	77. gleaming	78. glorious	79. gorgeous	80. graceful
81. greasy	82. grieving	83. perfect	84. responsive	85. petty
86. grumpy	87. handsome	88. happy	89. healthy	90. helpful
91. helpless	92. high	93. hollow	94. homely	95. horrific
96. huge	97. hungry	98. hurt	99. icy	100. ideal

08

VERBS

(ACTION WORD)

A **verb** is a <u>word</u> or a combination of words that indicates action or a state of being or condition. A verb is the part of a <u>sentence</u> that tells us what the subject performs. Verbs are the hearts of English sentences.

Examples:

- Ahaan <u>walks</u> in the morning. (A usual action)
- Shivika <u>is going</u> to school. (A condition of action)
- Avani <u>does not like</u> to walk. (A negative action)
- Dhara <u>is</u> a good girl. (A state of being)

Verbs are related to a lot of other factors like the *subject, person, number, tense, mood, voice,* etc.

Basic Forms of Verbs

There are **five basic** forms of verbs. These forms are as follows:

- **Base form:** Children <u>play</u> in the field.
- **Infinitive:** Tell them not <u>to play</u>
- **Past tense:** They <u>played</u> football yesterday.
- **Past participle:** I have <u>eaten</u> a burger.
- **Present participle:** I saw them <u>playing</u> with him today.

AUXILIARY VERBS

1] **Main Verbs:** These are the verbs which take the position of main verbs only.

For example: write, come, eat, go, etc.

2] **Fundamental Verbs**: These are the verbs which occupy the position of main verbs as well as the helping verb in the sentences, either simultaneously or separately. These are only three such verbs in English, viz. do, be, and have.

For example: a) I do not do exercise regularly.

If acting is an auxiliary verb, they are called as Primary auxiliary verbs.

PRIMARY AUXILIARY VERBS:

The Auxiliary verbs which change according to the tenses, number and person of the subject are called primary helping verbs, which are do, be and have.

Be – be, is, are, am, was, were, being, been.

Have – have, has, had, having.

Do – do, does, did, doing, done.

SECONDARY AUXILLARY OR HELPING VERBS:

The verbs which help the main verb in the sentences to complete its meaning is called as helping or Auxiliary verb. They are also called as secondary Auxiliary verbs.

SHALL: It is used to express the future. (Used with first person- I, We)

SHOULD: It is used as a past tense of shall, to express duty, to express probability.

WILL: Used to express future, it is used to express willingness, for polite requests or invitations, to express determination.

WOULD: It is used as past tense of will, to determine a habitual activity in past, to express a wish or a preference, to express suggestion or a polite request.

CAN: It is used to express ability or capacity, sometimes express permission, express possibilities.

COULD: It is use as a past tense of can in indirect speech, it is used to talk about possible actions now or in the future (especially to make suggestion), to express ability in the past, sometimes could is used for a request as an alternative to would/ would be able to.

MAY: To express permission, to express a wish, to express possibility.

MIGHT: It is used as a past tense of 'may', used in question for asking permission, might implies more politeness than may, to express possibility in a lesser degree.

MUST:

It is used to express a necessity, a command or sometimes an assumption or conclusion, to express fixed Determination/ obligation.

OUGHT TO:

It is used to express a necessity, a command or sometimes an assumption or conclusion and is synonyms to should and must.

USED TO:

It is used to express discontinued habits or a past situation which contrasts with the present, to express past routine or habit.

WAS TO:

It is used to express some probability of action that could take place.

HAD TO:

It is used to express some action which actually took place, generally in extension of the action that is referred with was to.

EXERCISE 47

IDENTIFYING VERBS

Q83] Circle the verbs.

Bicycle	read	book	tell	story	looks
funny	cat	fun	plays	with	child
runs	around	take	glass	drinks	eat
ring	sounds	music	climb	sliding	path
leaves	falling	girl	friends	piano	flute
rise	think	table	sat	couch	put
chair	swim	ride	broom	read	wish
tree	work	car	sleep	try	pail
flower	find	make	bird	go	sit
couch	put	feet	dog	Bells	picture

Q84] Write the verb from each sentence.

1) Teddy holds his plushy. ___________   2) Meena eats a carrot. ___________   3) The kids laugh at the joker. ______   4) After supper, they clean the dishes. ___________   5) Later, take a bath. ___________   6) Leela looks sad. ___________   7) Even now, we are late. ___________   8) We often think about you. ___________   9) Bring me the bowl. ___________   10) Hold on for a minute. ___________

Q85] (A) Circle the verbs.

[walk   kitten   say   eat   water   fly   book   stop
paper   mouse   writes   sang   stood   blanket   pig]

(B) Complete the sentences using the verbs from above.

1. I _____________ an apple every day.

2. Let's _____________ for some ice cream.

3. We _____________ still for our picture.

4. Rocky _____________ letters to his cousin.

5. We _____________ to the playground after school.

6. The singer _____________ a sad song.

Q86] (A) Circle the verbs.

[bear   swim   reads   parrot   sister   called   grass   hop
catch   tennis   raked   fell   smile   shoe   door]

(B) Complete the sentences using the verbs from above.

1. I __________ every ball that I can.

2. The teacher __________ us a book.

3. We __________ when we are happy.

4. Rabbits __________ across the field.

5. My aunt __________ me on my birthday.

6. The clown __________ off of his chair.

Q87] (A) Circle the verbs.

[sitting   dog   pick   car   came   looks   chases   balloon   eat
pink   shirt   walk   told   toy   reads]

(B) Complete the sentences using the verbs from above.

1. The cat _____________ the mouse.

2. The children _____________ to the park.

3. The teacher _________ the class a story.

4. Mom ________ the kids to _________up their toys.

5. My friend ________ to my house after school.

6. The girls ______ pie while __________ at the table.

<u>EXERCISE 48</u>

SINGULAR AND PLURAL VERBS

Singular subjects use singular verbs: The girl walks.

Plural subjects use plural verbs: The girls walk.

Q88] [A] Circle the correct verb:

1) My uncle is / are making supper.
2) Your friends is / are nice.
3) Liana and Vincy eats / eat together often.
4) The teacher reads / read everyday to the children.
5) Students enjoys / enjoy playing outside.
6) Sharad is / are sharing his lunch.
7) My aunts lives / live nearby.
8) Your dogs likes / like to go for a walk.
9) My best friend is / are Arun.
10) Your dad is / are tall.

[B] Circle the correct verb:

1) The actor is / are old.

2) Mark and Lennon is / are singing.

3) Your friend is / are sad.

4) The steps is / are slippery.

5) The cushion is / are soft.

6) The pants is / are long.

7) The sweaters is / are warm.

8) The scarves protects / protect you from the cold.

9) The coat is / are short.

10) The shoes is / are black.

[C] Circle the correct verb:

1) Anderson eats / eat cake.

2) Praveer and Aditya prefers / prefer pie.

3) Maya and I likes / like soup.

4) Emily and you enjoys / enjoy salad more.

5) My mom makes / make great food.

6) Your dad is / are a good cook too.

7) I drinks / drink milk with my meal.

8) The boys drinks / drink water with their meal.

9) My friends has / have fruit juice.

10) The kitten licks / lick the cream.

EXERCISE 49

ACTION AND LINKING VERBS

Linking verbs are words that express a state of being: is, were, was

Q89] Draw a line under action verbs and circle linking verbs.

[**A**] 1. Sam is a dog.   2. The Mishras visited their grandparents. 3. Hari looks at the books.   4. They were afraid.   5. Geeta and Priyal played soccer last summer.   6. Your sisters are nice.   7. Mansi set the table.   8. Nikita and Samiksha danced all night.   9. The students wrote their name.   10. The teachers were proud of their students.

[**B**] 1. Purva peeled the potatoes.   2. Angel is happy.   3. I am tall. 4. Piyush grows wheat in his field.   5. Nancy cut her finger.   6. The teacher wrote on the board.   7. Cats are curious.   8. Commercials are annoying.   9. Danish picked up the phone.   10. Jay turned off the TV.

<u>EXERCISE 50</u>

CONJUGATING VERBS: 'TO BE'

Q90] Write the verbs:

Hint: am, is, are, was, were, been, being

I _______am_______   I _____was_____

We ______________   We ______________

You ______________   You ______________

He ______________   She ______________

They ______________   They ______________

I am _____being_____   I had _____been_____

We are ______________   We had ______________

You are ______________   You had ______________

He is ______________   She had ______________

They are ______________   They had ______________

'TO GO'

Q91] Write the verbs:

Hint: go, goes, went, going, gone

I _______go_______   I_______went_______

We ______________   We ______________

You ______________   You ______________

He ______________   She ______________

They ______________   They ______________

I am ______going______   I had ______gone______

We are ______________   We had ______________

You are ______________   You had ______________

He is ______________   She had ______________

They are ______________   They had ______________

EXERCISE 51

COMMONLY CONFUSED WORDS

IS AND ARE

Q92] Write 'is' or 'are'.

Hint: Use 'are' with we, you and they; Use 'is' with he, she and it.

1) Saniya ______________ happy to see us.

2) We ______________ on time for once.

3) The dog ______________ in the back yard.

4) You ______________ with your cousin Tom.

5) They ______________ impatient to enter the room.

6) He ______________ next in line.

7) My parents ______________ in the living room.

8) ______________ you upstairs?

9) We ______________ ready.

10) She ______________ the last one.

CAN - MAY

Q93] Write "can" or "may" in each sentence.

"Can" is used to show ability. "May" is the politest way to express permission.

1. I ______ write with both hands.

2.   You ___________ go to the bathroom.
3.   Your parents ___________ visit Amsterdam next winter.
4.   Kabir ___________ play the piano beautifully.
5.   ___________ I have the butter, please?
6.   She ___________ cook an amazing meal.
7.   You ___________ have a second helping of dessert.
8.   Yes, they ___________ play with their blocks in the living room.
9.   ___________ you put the leftovers in the refrigerator, please?
10.   ___________ I eat the last piece of pastry?

WILL- WOULD

"Will" is used for an action in the future: Jiya will go to the store tomorrow.

"Would" is used when an action may happen if something else happens: Jiya would go to the store if she had time.

"Would" can also be the past tense of will: Yesterday, Jiya said she would go to the store today.

Q94] Write "will" or "would" in each sentence.

1.   Tomorrow we ______ go to the movies.
2.   You ___________ finish your homework if you knew what to do.
3.   ___________ you pass me the salt?
4.   Falguni ___________ write his teacher a letter.
5.   You ___________ help your dad with this task.
6.   Your friend ___________ come to the show if he could.
7.   I ___________ like to go with you, if my mom says yes.
8.   You ___________ look both ways before crossing the street.
9.   They ___________ go on a vacation next year.
10.   Arpita said she ______ miss school today.

EXERCISE 52

Q95] [A] Circle the verbs.

[added   carrot   mixed   pulled   took   apple
decide   orange   ran   tuned   arranged   finished
painted   stopped   used   begin   helped   picks
story   unison   climbed   liked   practice   tarnished
zipper   extended]

[B] Use the verbs to complete the sentences.

1. The sailors pulled on the ropes and the sails ____________.
2. The firefighters put on their suits, drove to the fire and ____________ the tall ladder.
3. The hair stylist ____________ his scissors to cut the woman's hair.
4. The baker ____________ the flour and the water together before adding the eggs.
5. The florist cut the flowers and ____________ them into a nice bouquet.
6. The chef stirred his soup carefully, then ____________ more salt.
7. The artist ____________ a beautiful portrait of his subject.
8. The bus driver ____________ to let more people on the bus.
9. The doctor ____________ her patient's pulse before listening to his heart.
10. The coach ____________ the players learn a new strategy.
11. Every time the secretary ____________ up the phone, the line cuts off.
12. The musician ____________ her guitar before she began to play.

Q96] [A] Circle the verbs.

[prepared   hot   dogs   launched   supported   developed
passed   photo   played   created   computer   understand
theater   includes   seems   shed   rushed   groaned
airplane   realize   hiked]

[B] Complete the sentences using the verbs from above.

1. The meal ______________ two side dishes.
2. My uncle ________ to the store to get there before it closed.
3. I ______________ a very difficult math test last week.
4. We ___________ when we heard what dinner would be.
5. Aunt Sara ______________ an amazing video game.
6. The thick branches ______________ our tree house.
7. My little brother ______________ his model rocket yesterday.
8. Mary and I ___________ far into the woods to pick berries.
9. Dad ______________ thrilled with his new fishing boat.
10. Most dogs ______________ a lot of fur at least twice a year.
11. We ___________ the problem because it was explained well.
12. I _______ for our vacation by packing a week ahead of time.

Q97] [A] Circle the verbs.

[replaced   twirled   balloons   study   found   assembled
wired   laughs   candy   shook   involve   order
highlights   dictionary   dances   pitched   planted   pillow
spread   upgraded]

[B] Complete the sentences using the verbs from above.

1. My uncle ________ at all of my silly jokes.
2. The class ________ in the gym for a presentation.
3. It took a long time, but I ________ the hidden treasure.
4. Our teacher ________ the best parts of the book.
5. Nita ________ a curve ball, and we won the game.
6. Katrina ________ very well to rock music.
7. My mom ________ my computer for me.
8. She was so excited that she ________ around in circles.
9. I always ________ cream cheese on my bagels.

10.   Henry _______ with excitement when he got a new cellphone.

11.   The school _______ a beautiful flower garden.

12.   If I want to do well on the test, I _______ hard.

<u>EXERCISE 53</u>

PHRASAL VERBS

A phrasal verb is made of a verb plus another word like up, down, after, to, in, out, etc. Pick up, show off, get in, Walk out, get up, get in, cut off

They are also made of a verb plus a preposition another word like up, down, after, to, in, out, etc. Stand up, fill in, look into, grow up, count on

Q98] Underline the phrasal verb in each sentence.

[A] 1. Can someone <u>pick up</u> the phone?

2. You dad hung up the picture last night.

3. The children got off the playground climber and ran home.

4. His mom waved for him to get in the car.

5. The sitter looked after the children.

6. Sophia bent down to pick up her pencil.

7. The students stood up for the national anthem.

8. Will you invite your friend to sit down?

9. Elena walked in the room.

10. Put down your tablet; it's dinner time.

11. What time do you get up in the morning?

12. His uncle filled up the car with gasoline.

[B] 1. They called off the search. They found the cat.

2. We should cut back on sugar; we eat too much of it.

3. The man gave away his fortune.

4. Remember to hand in your assignment.

5. The cat knocked over the flower vase.

6. Don't leave out any detail.

7. She works so hard; she doesn't want to let her parents down.

8. The meeting is put off until next week.

9. The boy took apart the toy and found what was broken.

10. They carried out their orders.

11. Your Spanish teacher comes from South America.

12. The daughter takes after her mother.

[C] 1. Avni was brought up by his grandmother.

2. The contestant called on his friend for support.

3. Give her a call; she needs some cheering up.

4. Alex came up with the answer by himself.

5. The researcher came across some interesting findings.

6. Aunt Lalita dropped by for a visit.

7. Your friend dropped off your ball. You had left it at school.

8. Angela gave out the answer to her partners.

9. Don't give up; it will get easier.

10. The players hung out after the game.

11. Make sure you log off the computer when you are done.

12. You could look up the answer on Wikipedia.

EXERCISE 54

SUBJECT-VERB AGREEMENT

Q99] Write the form of the verb that agrees with the subject.

[A] 1.The children _______ Pokémon cards. (to collect)

2. Angela __________ ketchup on her eggs. (to put)

3. He __________ that I am a nice friend. (to think)

4. They __________ home after school. (to walk)

5. We __________ water instead of juice. It's better for us. (to drink)

6. I __________ with my mother every day. (to talk)

7. You __________ excellent spaghetti sauce. (to make)

8. She __________ really fast for her age. (to type)

9. It __________ like it will rain. (to look)

10. We __________ our bikes to our friend's house. (to ride)

11. He __________ his room every week. (to clean)

12. The teacher __________ the students while they work. (to observe)

[B] 1. He _______ in a hotel during his vacation. (to stay)

2. Your friend __________ to the pool every week. (to go)

3. He __________ the door to get inside. (to push)

4. They __________ their laundry every Thursday. (to wash)

5. Farida____________ many books in a month. (to read)

6. We usually ___________ everything that is on our plate. (to eat)

7. You ___________ that you can solve the problem. (to think)

8. She ___________ a new song every morning. (to sing)

9. They ___________ to another country in the summer. (to travel)

10. Your mother ___________ the best mayo and cheese. (to make)

11. Silver ___________ over time. (to tarnish)

12. Your brother ___________ too much television. (to watch)

[C] 1. The lights _______ on automatically. (to turn)

2. The phone ___________ three times before the answering machine picks up. (to ring)

3. James __________ his bed every day. (to make)

4. Kindness ___________ a long way with people. (to go)

5. Spring ___________ winter. (to follow)

6. Every day, they ___________ to put their books in their bag. (to remember)

7. We ____________ at the gym in the afternoon. (to exercise)

8. You ___________ your clothes by separate colors. (to sort)

9. I ___________ all the options before I write my answer. (to consider)

10. She __________ her teeth in the morning and at night. (to brush)

11. Her friend ___________ all the time. (to smile)

12. We ___________ at our desk when we are in the class. (to sit)

EXERCISE 55

HELPING VERBS: CAN AND COULD

Q100] Write "can" or "could" on the blank lines.

Hint: Can is used to express possibility, permission, willingness, and ability. Could is used to express a conditional tone, the past tense of can, and possibility.

1. She _______ do a cartwheel.
2. ____________ you clean the kitchen for me please?
3. ____________ I spend the night at Oscar's house on Friday?
4. For lunch, we ____________ have sandwiches or salads.
5. The teacher ____________ let you have a night with no homework.
6. ____________ we please stay up later than our normal bedtime?
7. ____________ you please give me a fork?
8. Payal ____________ have read the book in third grade.
9. The sun ____________ shine later this afternoon.
10. My friends ____________ have left the party early.
11. ____________ you please give me a hand with this math problem?
12. Studying for the test ____________ be a wise idea.

MAY, MIGHT AND MUST

Q101] Fill in the blank with may, might, or must.

Hint: May is used to express possibility or permission. Might is used to express a smaller possibility. Must is used to express a requirement.

1. The bus driver says we ____________ stay in our seats on the way to school.
2. There's a strong chance my dad ____________ play football with us after dinner.
3. Our math teacher ____________ give us a big surprise test, but I doubt it.

4. It _______________ snow later this afternoon according to the weather forecast.
5. In art class, we _______________ not put paint on our classmates.
6. The entire family _______________ fly to France if we win the lottery.
7. _______________ I please get a new video game?
8. Stacy studies all the time, so she _______________ get a great grade.
9. Scott doesn't study at all, but he still _______________ get a good grade.
10. We _______________ clean our rooms or else we will not be allowed to watch TV.

Q102] Choose the correct auxiliary verb:

Hint: An auxiliary verb is a verb that helps the main verb of the sentence

[A] 1. Kiara ______ working on his homework. (is / am / does / are)

2. Samantha ________ make dinner with her grandma. (is / am / does/ are)

3. The friends ________ going to South Carolina. (is / am / does / are)

4. ________ your dad work in this building? (is / am / does / are)

5. ________ you want to come to my house later? (are / am / do / does)

6. Mike __________ like animals. (isn't / doesn't / aren't / don't)

7. The poster ________ hanging on the wall. (is / am / does / are)

8. Where ________ your family like to eat? (are / am / do / does)

9. ________ your brother playing soccer this weekend? (is / am / does / are)

10. Patty ________ watching television anymore. (isn't / doesn't / aren't / don't)

11. His family _________ go to parties. (isn't / doesn't / aren't / don't)

12. Tony and Tracy ________ planning a vacation. (is / am / does / are)

[B] 1. The teachers _________ planning a field trip. (is / am / does / are)

2. Our car ________ make a strange sound. (is / am / does / are)

3. My friend ________ having a party. (is / am / does / are)

4. ________ your parents have a lot of friends? (Is / Do / Does / Are)

5. ________ your dog eat a lot of food? (Is / Do / Does / Are)

6. My mom ________ cook dinner. (isn't / doesn't / aren't / don't)

7. The school ________ closing on Friday. (is / am / do / are)

8. What ________ your cats like to play? (is / am / do / are)

9. ________ your friends in the fourth grade? (Is / Do / Does / Are)

10. Isha _______ studying French this year. (isn't / doesn't / aren't / don't)

11. We ________ like going to bed early. (isn't / doesn't / aren't / don't)

12. Ricky ________ dancing in the next show. (is / am / does / are)

[C] 1. Our principal ________ working hard. (is / am / does / are)

2. My house ________ have three bedrooms. (is / am / does / are)

3. My parents ________ going to a restaurant. (is / am / do / are)

4. ________ your cat like to play with yarn? (Is / Do / Does / Are)

5. ______ your friends want to come over to play? (Is / Do / Does / Are)

6. My grandparents ________visit us. (isn't / doesn't / aren't / don't)

7. The bus drivers ________ driving on Monday. (is / am / do / are)

8. What ________Randy like to do? (is / am / does / are)

9. ________ your teacher helping you read? (Is / Do / Does / Are)

10. Carl and Harry _________ writing their book reports. (isn't / doesn't / aren't / don't)

11. She _________ run very fast. (isn't / doesn't / aren't / don't)

12. Sophia and Ivira _________ talking about their favorite classes. (is / am / do / are)

TENSES

TENSES	STRUCTURE OF VERB	EXAMPLE
1) SIMPLE PRESENT TENSE	**base verb (-s, -es, -ies)**	- Jay **takes** him to school.
2) PRESENT CONTINUOUS TENSE	**am/is/are + V1 + ing**	- Jay **is taking** him to school. - Jay & Anu **are taking** him to school.
3) PRESENT PERFECT TENSE	**has/have + past participle(V3)**	- Jay **has taken** him to school. - Jay and Anu **have taken** him to school. - I **have taken** him to school.
4) PRESENT PERFECT CONTINUOUS TENSE	**has/have + been + V1 + ing**	- Rama **has been taking** him to school. - They **have been taking** him to school.
5) SIMPLE PAST TENSE	**Past tense of the base verb (-d,-ed,-ied)**	- Jay **took** him to school.
6) PAST CONTINUOUS TENSE	**was/were + V1 + ing**	- Jay **was taking** him to school. - Kim & Jay **were taking** him to school.
7) PAST PERFECT TENSE	**had + past participle (V3)**	- Jay **had taken** him to school. - They **had taken** him to school.

8) PAST PERFECT CONTINUOUS TENSE	**had + been + V1 + ing**	- Jay **had been taking** him to school. - They **had been taking** him to school.
9) SIMPLE FUTURE TENSE	**will / shall + V1**	- Jay **shall take** him to school.
10) FUTURE CONTINUOUS TENSE	**will be / shall be + V1 +ing**	- Jay & I **will be taking** him to school.
11) FUTURE PERFECT TENSE	**will/ shall + have + past participle (V3)**	- Jay **shall have taken** him to school.
12) FUTURE PERFECT CONTINUOUS TENSE	**will/shall + have + been + verb + ing**	- Jay & Anu **will have been taking** him to school.

Note:

1] In present tense:

a) 'am' is used with 'I', 'is' used with singulars and 'are' used with plurals only.

b) In simple present tense, the formula (-s,-es,-ies) is applicable only with singular name, he or she. V1 form (base verb) is applied to the rest (I, you, we, they).

c) 'Has' is used with singular and 'have' is used with plural.

d) 'Have' will be used with 'I' & 'You'.

2] In past tense:

a) 'Was' is used with singular, while 'were' is used with plural.

b) 'Had' is used with both singular and plural.

3] In future tense:

a) Shall is used with 1st person (I & We).

b) Will is used for the 2nd and 3rd person (You, He/She, They).

IRREGULAR VERBS

Infinitive	Past Simple	Past Participle
be	was/were	been
beat	beat	beaten
become	became	become
begin	began	begun
bite	bit	biten
blow	blew	blown
break	broke	broken
bring	brought	brought
build	built	built
buy	bought	bought
catch	caught	caught
choose	chose	chosen
come	came	come
cost	cost	cost
cut	cut	cut
do	did	done
draw	drew	drawn
dream	dreamt(-ed)	dream(-ed)
drink	drank	drunk
drive	drove	driven
eat	ate	eaten
fall	fell	fallen
feed	fed	fed
feel	felt	felt
fight	fought	fought
find	found	found
fly	flew	flown
forget	forgot	forgotten
forgive	forgave	forgiven
freeze	froze	frozen
get	got	got
give	gave	given
go	went	gone
grow	grew	grown
hang	hung	hung
have	had	had
hear	heard	heard
hide	hid	hidden
hit	hit	hit
hold	held	held
hurt	hurt	hurt
keep	kept	kept
know	knew	known
lay	laid	laid
lead	led	led
leave	left	left
lend	lent	lent
let	let	let
lie	lay	lain
light	lit	lit

Infinitive	Past Simple	Past Participle
lose	lost	lost
make	made	made
mean	meant	meant
meet	met	met
pay	paid	paid
put	put	put
read	read[red*]	read[red*]
ride	rode	ridden
ring	rang	rung
rise	rose	risen
run	ran	run
say	said	said
see	saw	saw
seek	sought	sought
sell	sold	sold
send	sent	sent
set	set	set
sew	sewed	sewn/sewed
shake	shook	shaken
shine	shone	shone
shoot	shot	shot
show	showed	shown/ showed
shrink	shrank	shrunk
shut	shut	shut
sing	sang	sung
sink	sank	sunk
sit	sat	sat
sleep	slept	slept
smell	smelt	smelt
speak	spoke	spoken
spend	spent	spent
spread	spread	spread
stand	stood	stood
steal	stole	stolen
stick	stuck	stuck
strike	struck	struck
swim	swam	swum
swing	swung	swung
take	took	taken
teach	taught	taught
tear	tore	torn
tell	told	told
think	thought	thought
throw	threw	thrown
understand	understood	understood
wake	woke	woken
wear	wore	worn
win	won	won
write	wrote	written

PRESENT TENSE

Sr. no	Tenses	Affirmative	Negative	Interrogative	Negative Interrogative
1	Simple Present Tense	I/we/you/they write an article everyday. He/she writes an article everyday.	I/we/they don't write an article everyday. He/she doesn't write an article everyday.	Do I/we/you/they write an article everyday? Does he/she write an article everyday?	Don't I/we/you/they write an article everyday? Doesn't he/she write an article everyday?
2	Present Tense 'To Be'	I am a teacher. You are a teacher. He/she is a teacher We/they are teachers.	I am not a teacher. You aren't a teacher. He/she isn't a teacher. We/they aren't teachers.	Am I a teacher? Are you a teacher? Is he/she a teacher? Are we/they teachers?	Am I not a teacher? Aren't you a teacher? Isn't he/she a teacher? Aren't we/they teachers?
3	Present Tense 'To Have'	I/we/they have a laptop. He/she has a laptop.	I/we/they don't have a laptop. He/she doesn't have a laptop.	Do I/we/they have a laptop? Does he/she have a laptop?	Don't I/we/they have a laptop? Doesn't He/she have a laptop?

Sr. no	Tenses	Affirmative	Negative	Interrogative	Negative Interrogative
4	Present Continuous Tense	I'm writing an article now. He/she is writing an article now. We/you/they are writing an article now.	I'm not writing an article now. He/she isn't writing an article now. We/you/they aren't writing an article now.	Am I writing an article now? Is he/she writing an article now? Are we/you/they writing an article now?	Am I not writing an article now? Isn't he/she writing an article now? Aren't we/you/they writing an article now?
5	Present Perfect Tense	I/we/you/they have written an article. He/she have written an article.	I/we/you/they haven't written an article. He/she haven't written an article.	Have I/we/you/they written an article? Has he/she written an article?	Haven't I/we/you/they written an article? Hasn't he/she written an article?
6	Present Perfect Continuous	I/we/you/they have been writing an article. He/she have been writing an article.	I/we/you/they haven't been writing an article. He/she haven't been writing an article.	Have I/we/you/they been writing an article? Has he/she been writing an article?	Haven't I/we/you/they been writing an article? Hasn't he/she been writing an article?

EXERCISE 56

Q103) Simple Present Tense
Fill in the blanks with the correct form of the verbs given in brackets.

1. She .... (go) to her office with a friend.
2. Why you .... (like) movies?
3. My friend .... (visit) his grandmother every day.
4. (do) Ritesh .... (love) the cold weather?
5. .... (do) you .... (plan) to visit Kashmir this year?
6. We always .... (have) an early dinner.
7. His parents .... (plan) a trip abroad every six months.
8. Our doctor in the neighbourhood .... (make) a lot of money.
9. I .... (help) my mother sometimes.
10. Sheetal .... (come) here every Sunday.
11. We .... (eat) rice for dinner every day.
12. He never .... (hide) the truth.
13. Make hay while the sun .... (shine)
14. Apples .... (be) good for health.
15. The dogs .... (bark) every night.

Q104) Present Continuous Tense
Fill in the blanks with the correct form of the verbs given in brackets.

1. The CAs ___________(make) a lot of money these days.
2. Why _______(be) he _________(not help) you?
3. ___________(be) you ___________(come) to my house today?
4. The band ___________(play) all the old songs.
5. His parents ___________(visit) him today evening.
6. Vijay ___________(behave) very foolishly.
7. By ignoring the traffic signal, they ___________(break) the law.
8. It ___________(rain) heavily outside.
9. Our cook ___________(not come) today.

10. We ___________(face) a lot of problems in our society these days.
11. The driver ____________(plan) to take off tomorrow.
12. I ____________(come) to the party tonight.
13. The children ____________(play) hide and seek in the garden.
14. The train ____________(run) late.
15. Today, the sun __________(shine) bright.
16. Farmers ____________(plucking) berries from the bushes.

Q105) Present Perfect Tense
Fill in the blanks with the correct form of the verbs given in brackets.

1. The cat .... (drink) all the milk.
2. They .... (not arrive) yet.
3. She .... (not qualify) the written test.
4. We .... (be) already .... (see) the movie.
5. I .... (think) of inviting all my friends.
6. My brother .... (not see) the Red Fort yet.
7. The teacher .... (has) just ....
(enter) the class.
8. Rajeev .... (stop) learning piano.
9. The media .... (has) just ....
(leave) the premises.
10. My parents .... (has/have) recently
.... (celebrate) their fifteenth anniversary.
11. Rakesh .... (lose) the way.
12. The robbers .... (murder) three persons.
13. The minister ....(has) already ....
(deliver) his speech.
14. The Sadhus .... (chant) the mantras.
15. Her mother .... (has) not ....
(rest).
16. The thief .... (run away).

Q106) Present Perfect Continuous Tense
Fill in the blanks with the correct form of the verbs given in brackets.

1. It .... (rain) since morning.
2. We .... (wait) for Rajeev for more than an hour now.
3. Sheela .... (practice) badminton for three hours.
4. This statue .... (lying) here for ages.
5. Parul .... (talk) on the phone for almost one hour.
6. The court .... (send) the summons for three weeks.
7. The teachers .... (invigilate) for three hours.
8. These children .... (suffer) from this allergy for the past one year.
9. I .... (clean) the classroom since morning.
10. My mother .... (visit) temples for two weeks now.
11. This playground .... (lying) in disuse for the past three months.
12. The man in the next room .... (sing) at 6 o'clock in the morning.
13. I can't sleep in her room anymore. She .... (snore) all through.
14. Saheb's family .... (wait) at the bus stop since 8 a.m.
15. The patient .... (sneeze) non-stop.
16. The bikers .... (race) since the afternoon.

PAST TENSE

1	Simple Past Tense	I/we/you/ he/she/ they wrote an article yesterday.	I/we/you/ he/ she/ they didn't write an article yesterday.	Did I/we/ you/he/she/ they write an article yesterday?	Didn't I/we/ you/he/she/ they write an article yesterday?
2	Past Tense 'To Be'	-I/he/she was a teacher last year. -We/You/ they were teachers last year.	-I/he/she wasn't a teacher last year. -We/You/ they weren't teachers last year.	- Was I/ he/she a teacher last year? Were we/ you/they teachers last year?	- Wasn't I/ he/she a teacher last year? Weren't we/ you/they teachers last year?
3	Past Tense 'To Have'	I/we/you/ he/ she/they had a laptop last month.	I/we/you/he/ she/ they didn't have a laptop last month.	Did I/we/ you/he/she/ they have a laptop last month?	Didn't I/we/ you/he /she/ they have a laptop last month?
4	Past Continuous Tense	I/he/she was writing an article yesterday. You/we/they were writing an article yesterday.	I/he/she wasn't writing an article yesterday. You/we/ they weren't writing an article yesterday.	Was I/he/ she writing an article yesterday? Were you/ we/they writing an article yesterday?	Wasn't I/he/ she writing an article yesterday? Weren't you/we/ they writing an article yesterday?
5	Past Perfect Tense	I/we/you/ he/she/they had written an article yesterday.	I/we/you/ he/she/they hadn't written an article yesterday.	Had I/we/ you/ he/she/ they written an article yesterday?	Hadn't I/we/ you/ he/she/ they written an article yesterday?

6	Past Perfect Continuous	I/we/you/ he/she/they had been writing an article yesterday.	I/we/you/ he/she/they hadn't been writing an article yesterday.	Had I/we/ you/ he/she/ they been writing an article yesterday?	Hadn't I/ we/you/he/ she/they been writing an article yesterday?

Q107) Simple past tense
Fill in the blanks with the correct form of the verbs given in brackets.

1. We .... (eat) chocolates as a dessert in the party.
2. Kalpana Chawla .... (join) NASA as an astronaut.
3. Rowdy students .... (break) the furniture of the school last week.
4. I .... (live) in the hostel for five years.
5. Sheela's younger brother .... (finish) his homework in the morning.
6. The teacher .... (give) a prize to the topper.
7. The dignitaries .... (welcome) the guests.
8. The driver of the car .... (apply) the brakes.
9. We .... (go) to a restaurant for dinner.
10. A massive fire .... (break) out in the building yesterday.
11. The educationists .... (plan) the syllabus as per the guidelines.
12. Twenty-five jawans .... (die) in the avalanche.
13. My father .... (buy) an expensive SUV a few days back.
14. The waiter .... (clear) the tables after dinner.
15. He never .... (lose) sight of the goal.
16. The train .... (shake) violently before getting derailed.

Q108) Past Continuous tense

Fill in the blanks with the correct form of the verbs given in brackets.

1. She .... (watch) a movie on television in her bedroom.
2. The thief .... (break) the lock when he was caught.
3. Seema .... (cook) when the guests entered.
4. What .... (be) you .... (do) at the railway station?
5. .... (be) he .... (listen) to the shlokas at the temple?
6. Prem .... (play) the instrument when his tutor came.
7. I .... (be) busy (wash) clothes when my friend came.
8. The phone .... (ring) when the watchman was sleeping.
9. When I went to my friends' place, they .... (sleep).
10. The girl .... (drown) when the boatmen saw her.
11. Why .... (be) you .... (jump) on the road?
12. The Principal .... (give away) prizes when the dance troupe came.
13. Where .... (be) you .... (go) when your mother spotted you?
14. Why .... (be) she not .... (wear) her raincoat when it was raining outside?
15. They .... (have) their breakfast when the power went off.
16. The children .... (not pay) attention in the class.

Q109) Past perfect tense
Fill in the blanks with the correct form of the verbs given in brackets.

1. Why .... (has/have) you .... (not catch) the thief earlier?
2. The king .... (leave) before the prince came.
3. My mother .... (finish) her chores before everybody woke up.
4. The waiter .... (serve) the coffee after everyone finished their meals.
5. .... (has/have) you .... (make) it on time, you would have got the job?
6. We .... (go) to Manali before the summer approached.
7. When they .... (enter) the room, the music started.
8. My friend .... (purchase) the tickets before the distribution closed.
9. Where .... (has) you .... (go) when I called you up yesterday.
10. The doctor .... (instruct) the nurses to take special care of the old patients.
11. The bus driver .... (leave) the bus before it met with an accident.
12. In my childhood, my father would take me to places that I .... (has/have) not .... (visit)
13. The culprit .... (has) been .... (thrash) before the police arrived.
14. .... (Has/Have) he not .... (work) hard, he would have failed.
15. Where .... (have) you .... (disappear) when there was a party yesterday?
16. The children .... (have pluck) all the flowers before the arrival of the gardener.

Q110) Past perfect continuous tense
Fill in the blanks with the correct form of the verbs given in brackets.

1. Sita .... (has) been .... (sit) at the computers for five hours when the bell rang.
2. The doctors .... (has) been .... (attend) to the patients when they heard noises outside.
3. The laborers........................ (has) been .... (dig) the site when the wall came off.
4. Poorvi .... (watch) the television when the earthquake came.
5. Parents .... (attend) the counseling session when the electricity went off.
6. The secretary .... (look) at the files since morning when the fire alarm rang.
7. He .... (play) guitar for almost five hours when his tutor came.
8. Children .... (splash) water in the pool for over three hours.
9. Parents .... (worry) about their sick son all day.
10. The typist .... (manage) her work for a long time.
11. Children .... (play) in the garden since dawn.
12. The car driver .... (speed) for quite some time.
13. The grandmother .... (sit) in the sun for an hour.
14. The child .... (sleep) in the Verandah for three hours.
15. It .... (rain) cats and dogs since morning.
16. Why he not .... (study) geography in school for so many days?

FUTURE TENSE

Sr. no	Tenses	Affirmative	Negative	Interrogative	Negative Interrogative
1	Simple Future Tense	I/we shall write an article tomorrow. You/he/she/they will write an article tomorrow.	I/we shalln't write an article tomorrow. You/he/she/ they won't write an article tomorrow.	Shall I/we/ write an article tomorrow? Won't you/he/she/they write an article tomorrow?	Shalln't I/we write an article tomorrow? Won't you/he/she they write an article tomorrow?
2	Future Tense 'To Be'	-I/we shall be a teacher tomorrow. -You/he/she/they will be a teacher tomorrow.	-I/we shalln't a teacher tomorrow. - You/he/she/ they won't be a teacher tomorrow.	-Shall I/we be a teacher tomorrow? Will you/he/she/ they be a teacher tomorrow?	- Shalln't I/we be a teacher tomorrow? -Won't you/he/she/they be a teacher tomorrow?
3	Future Tense 'To Have'	I/we shall have a laptop next month. You/he/she/they will have a laptop next month.	I/we shalln't have a laptop next month. You/he/she/they won't have a laptop next month.	Shalln't I/we have have a laptop next month? Won't you/he/she/they have a laptop next month?	Shalln't I/we have have a laptop next month? Won't you/he/she/they have a laptop next month?

Sr. no	Tenses	Affirmative	Negative	Interrogative	Negative Interrogative
4	Future Continuous Tense	I/we/shall be writing an article tomorrow. He/she/they will be writing an article tomorrow.	I/we shalln't be writing an article tomorrow. He/she/they won't be writing an article tomorrow.	Shall I/we be writing an article tomorrow? Will he/she/they be writing an article tomorrow?	Shalln't I/we be writing an article tomorrow? Won't he/she/they be writing an article tomorrow?
5	Future Perfect Tense	I/we shall have written an article tomorrow. You/He/she/they will have written an article tomorrow.	I/we/shalln't have written an article tomorrow. You/He/she/they will have written an article tomorrow.	Shall I/we have written an article tomorrow? Will you/he/she/they have written an article tomorrow?	Shalln't I/we have written an article tomorrow? Won't he/she/they have written an article tomorrow?
6	Future Perfect Continuous	I/we/shall have been writing an article tomorrow. He/she/they will have been writing an article tomorrow.	I/we/shalln't have been writing an article tomorrow. He/she/they won't have been writing an article tomorrow.	shall I/we have been writing an article tomorrow? Will He/she/they have been writing an article tomorrow?	Shalln't I/we have been writing an article tomorrow? Won't He/she/they have been writing an article tomorrow?

Q111) Simple Future Tense
Fill in the blanks with the correct form of the verbs given in brackets.

1. Mumbai Indians team .... (play) against Pune Supergiants on Thursday.
2. I .... (leave) for Kolkata next week.
3. The children .... (go) for a picnic tomorrow.
4. The prizes .... (be) distributed after the exams.
5. .... we place the order?
6. Why .... (he tell) a lie?
7. My father .... (buy) the lottery ticket in the evening.
8. I .... (not eat) my dinner tonight.
9. She .... (recite) the poem in her school.
10. Ramesh .... (resolve) the issue.
11. Poorvi .... (attend) the wedding next Sunday.
12. My parents .... (visit) the shrine tomorrow.
13. You .... (receive) your books through courier.
14. I .... (not visit) the doctor today.
15. Prerna .... (tie) Rakhee to her stepbrother also.
16. Raju .... (finish) his work by noon.

Q112) Future continuous tense
Fill in the blanks with the correct form of the verbs given in brackets.

1. She .... (help) her mother in the kitchen.
2. The organisers .... (introduce) the guests at the function.
3. The florist .... (deliver) the bouquet by afternoon.
4. Sunita .... (do) her homework shortly.
5. I .... (watch) the match tonight.
6. My parents .... (arrive) by the morning flight tomorrow.
7. India .... (soon compete) with the superpowers.
8. He .... (turn) eighteen next month.

9. The officials .... (visit) the school in the morning.
10. She is vomiting. She .... (fall) sick anytime.
11. Gopal .... (drive) all the way to Kanpur.
12. My brother .... (leave) for his foreign assignment in a day or two.
13. When .... you be .... participate in the competition?
14. I .... (wait) for you downstairs.
15. The movie .... (releasing) next Friday.
16. The principal .... (address) a group of parents on Saturday.

Q113) Future perfect tense
Fill in the blanks with the correct form of the verbs given in brackets.

1. I .... (decide) to leave by tomorrow morning.
2. She .... (finish) her cooking by the time I reach her place.
3. The thieves .... (steal) the money by the time the police arrives.
4. By next week, he .... (quit) his job.
5. In the coming years, doctors .... (discover) a cure for cancer.
6. The tournament .... (begin) by then.
7. In another ten years, bullet trains .... (become) a common sight.
8. The judge .... (pass) the judgment by afternoon.
9. The minister .... (visit) the shrine by 6 o'clock.
10. The train .... (reach) the station by the time we reach.
11. The doctors .... (perform) the operation seeing the condition of the patient.
12. The priest .... (finish) the prayers before more people gathered at the church.

13. The lioness .... (attack) its prey to feed its cubs.
14. He .... (return) the book by tomorrow morning.
15. The king .... (visit) the palace before the arrival of the enemies.

Question 114) Future Perfect Continuous tense
Fill in the blanks with the correct form of the verbs given in brackets.

1. I .... (revise) my syllabus by the end of the term.
2. He .... (Play) with his friends for nearly 3 hours.
3. The labourers .... (dig) the pit for close to five hours.
4. Shyam .... (reach) by evening time.
5. The postman .... (deliver) the parcel next week.
6. .... (will) you .... (run) the marathon tomorrow morning for six hours?
7. We .... (see) the 'London Bridge' by tonight.
8. I .... (do) the shopping for almost the entire day.
9. You .... (celebrate) your anniversary tomorrow.
10. Tomorrow, at this time we .... (drive) to Haridwar for three hours.
11. My mother .... (prepare) for a party next week this time.
12. When you meet me next, I .... (complete) my research shortly.
13. He .... (play) chess with his friend tomorrow.
14. The sun .... (set) by the time we finish our work.

15.   We .... (shop) in Mumbai tomorrow, when you reach here.
16.   My uncle .... (cover) the distance to Nainital before we reach there.

<u>EXERCISE 59</u>

PAST, PRESENT OR FUTURE TENSE?

Q115] [A] Write past, present, or future for each sentence.

1)   Max eats his vegetables every day. ____________
2)   The students listened to the lesson. ____________
3)   Dad will clean the kitchen tonight. ____________
4)   Emily looks happy. ____________
5)   Tomorrow, it will snow. ____________
6)   He climbed the stairs last night. ____________
7)   Most children like the new park. ____________
8)   You will finish this later. ____________
9)   Mom liked her gift. ____________
10) The teacher will look at the homework. ____________

[B] Write past, present, or future for each sentence.

1)   The teacher reads a story every day. ____________
2)   Manny listens to the teacher. ____________
3)   Emma finished her sheet before me. ____________
4)   Look at the blue sky. ____________
5)   Tomorrow will be better. ____________
6)   Natalie will eat her dessert after dinner. ____________
7)   Last night, we watched TV. ____________
8)   Her hair is long. ____________
9)   The toys lay on the floor. ____________
10) The snow will stop tomorrow. ____________

[C] Write past, present, or future for each sentence.

1) More people like winter. ___________
2) You will like the pie. ___________
3) Dad liked last night's meal. ___________
4) We live in the country. ___________
5) My friend lived in the city. ___________
6) One day, I will live near a lake. ___________
7) Yesterday, we walked to school. ___________
8) Will you walk the dog? ___________
9) I walk often. ___________
10) I will show you, my project. ___________

NOTE: Tenses play an important role in sentence formation. Thus, it is suggested to learn the formulae of the tenses thoroughly.

RECOMMENDATION:

(I) You may get a lot of sentences and worksheets to practice on Google or in several other resources. Please try to practice the conversion of tenses from one form to another.

(II) Daily life sentences which you speak in your regional language, convert them into English sentences by detecting and applying the appropriate tense.

<u>EXERCISE 60</u>

PROGRESSIVE (continuous) VERB TENSES

Q116] Fill in the chart.

Verb	Past progressive	Present progressive	Future progressive
walk	was walking	is walking	will be walking
talk	___________	___________	___________
finish	___________	___________	___________
think	___________	___________	___________

	Past Continuous	Present Continuous	Future Continuous
circle			
eat			
hunt			
run			
play			
speak			
answer			
read			
fish	was fishing	is fishing	will be fishing
color			
write			
ride			
climb			
drink			
look			
share			
slide			
sleep			
visit			
snore			
make	was making	is making	will be making
bake			
cook			
freeze			
place			
put			
drop			
cut			
flip			
grill			
fry			
save			

10

ADVERBS

An adverb describes a verb, an adjective or another adverb. It tells us how, where, when, howmuch and with what frequency.

an adverb can tell...

HOW?

Quietly, peacefully, carefully, slowly, badly, closely, easily,

Well, fastly, quickly, cheerfully, efficiently, painfully, secretly

WHERE?

above, abroad, far, away, back, here, outside, backwards, behind, below, down, indoors, downstairs, inside, nearby, there, towards

WHEN?

now, yesterday, soon, later, tomorrow, yet, already, tonight, today, then, last, mosth, last, year

HOW MUCH?

quite, fairly, too, enormously, entirely, very, extremely, rather, almost, absolutely, just, barely, completely, enough, deeply, enormously, fully

HOW OFTEN?

always, sometimes, often, frequently, normally, generally, usually, occasionally, seldom, rarely, hardly, ever, never

What is an Adverb?

Adverbs are words that are used in sentences to describe or change the meaning of a Verb or Adjective or even another Adverb. They add a description to the sentence to make it more detailed and interesting. For example:

- *He ran **slowly** across the square.*

Here, one can see that the Adverb 'slowly' is describing the Verb 'ran' by telling that the person was running slowly.

Types of Adverbs

Adverbs are used in sentences to answer many questions about the Verbs/Adjectives/Adverbs themselves. The different types of Adverbs are as following:

Adverb of Time

E.g.: *The results were <u>announced</u> **yesterday**.*

Here the Adverb is **yesterday** which is answering the question: **When** were the results <u>announced?</u> 'Announced' is the verb in this sentence.

Adverb of Place

E.g.: *In spring, flowers <u>bloom</u> **everywhere**.*

Here the Verb is <u>bloom</u> and the Adverb is **everywhere,** answering the question: **Where** do the flowers <u>bloom</u> in spring?

Adverb of Manner

What is an <u>adverb of manner</u>? Look at examples below:

E.g.: *He **quietly** <u>slipped</u> away.*

The Adverb here is **quietly** which is telling the way or manner in which the action was carried out and the Verb is <u>slipped</u> which is telling: **How** did he <u>slip</u> away.

An adverb of manner is an adverb (such as strongly or slowly) that describes how and in what way the action of a verb is carried out.

FORMING ADVERBS FROM ADJECTIVES:

1. In a large number of cases, the adverb can be formed by simply adding '- ly' to the adjective.

ADJECTIVE	ADVERB
Cheap	Cheaply
Quick	Quickly
Strong	Strongly

2. If the adjective ends in with 'y', replace the 'y' with an 'i' and add '-ly'.

ADJECTIVE	ADVERB
Ready	Readily
Merry	Merrily
Easy	Easily

3. If the adjective ends with '- le', replace the 'e' at the end with 'y'.

ADJECTIVE	ADVERB
Understandable	Understandably
Forcible	Forcibly
Possible	Possibly

4. If the adjective ends with '-ic', add '-ally'. An exception: public -> publicly

ADJECTIVE	ADVERB
Idiotic	Idiotically
Tragic	Tragically
Basic	Basically

5. Some adjectives do not change form at all.

ADJECTIVE	ADVERB
Fast	Fast
Straight	Straight
Hard	Hard

6. In a large number of the cases, the adverb can be formed by simply adding '-ly' to the adjective.

Adverb of Frequency

What are <u>adverbs of frequency</u>? Let take a look at those examples below:

E.g.: *He likes to <u>watch</u> TV **every day.***

Here, the Adverb is **every day** and it is telling about the amount of time spent in doing the Verb, which is <u>watch</u>. The question in this sentence is: **How often** does he watch TV?

Adverbs of Frequency always tell us how often something takes place either in definite or indefinite terms.

Adverbs of Indefinite Frequency

100%	ALWAYS	It's **always** cold in this room.
90%	USUALLY	I **usually** get home about 6 o'clock.
80%	NORMALLY / GENERALLY	She doesn't **normally** arrive until ten.
70%	OFTEN / FREQUENTLY	I don't **often** drink beer.
50%	SOMETIMES	I **sometimes** think I'm going mad.
30%	OCCASIONALLY	I see him **occasionally** in town.
10%	SELDOM	I **seldom** read the newspaper.
5%	RARELY	We **rarely** / **hardly** ever go to concerts
0%	NEVER	We've **never** been to New York.

Adverbs of Definite Frequency

- Adverbs of definite frequency occur at the beginning or the end of a sentence.
- An adverb that describes definite frequency is one such as weekly/every week, daily/every day, or yearly/every year, once a month, twice a year, four times a day, every other week, etc.

FOR EXAMPLE:

- The library is open **every day.**
- He visits his grandpapa **every two weeks.**
- The moon waxes and wanes **every month.**
- This medicine is to be taken **hourly.**

> - Subject + *adverb* + main verb
> - Subject + Auxiliary verb + *adverb* + main verb
> - Subject + to be + *adverb*

Adverbs of Degree

E.g.: *She **almost** <u>finished</u> the work.*

The Verb here is <u>finished</u> and the Adverb is **almost** which is telling us about the amount of the work finished. The question being asked is: **How much** of the work did she finish?

Adverbs of Confirmation and Negation

E.g.: *They will **certainly** <u>like</u> this vase.*

The Adverb here is **certainly** which is reinforcing the Verb <u>like</u> in answer to the question: **Will** they like this vase?

Other examples of Adverbs of Confirmation are – Definitely, Absolutely, Surely, etc. Examples for Adverbs of Denial or Negation are – No, Don't, Can't, etc.

Adverbs of Comment

These Adverbs are used to make a comment on the entire sentence. They give a look at the speaker's viewpoint or opinion about the sentence. These Adverbs don't just change or describe the Verb; they influence the whole sentence.

Unfortunately, they found his secret easily.

Here, we see that adding the Adverb, unfortunately, has changed the entire tone of the sentence. Earlier, it was a passive tone, now it has a negative or disappointed tone.

Other examples of Adverbs of Comment are:

- *Luckily, the dog did not bite the children.*
- *Happily, the power returned before the big match.*

Adverbs of Conjunction

These Adverbs are used to connect ideas or clauses, they are used to show consequence or effect or the relation between the two clauses. To use these Adverbs to conjugate two clauses you need to use a semicolon (;) to connect them.

Clause 1: *He was going for an important interview.*

Clause 2: *He made sure he reached on time.*

He was going for an important interview; **accordingly**, he made sure he reached on time.

Here, we see how the Adverb '**accordingly**' is joining the two clauses and showing the relation between them with the use of a semicolon (;). Accordingly means- therefore or that is why.

A few other Adverbs of Conjunction are:

- **However** – Yet, on the other hand, in spite of
- **Consequently** – As a result, resulting in
- **Moreover** – Besides, in addition
- **Conversely** – Opposite of, contrary to

Position of Adverbs

What is the correct place to put an adverb in English sentences?

Adverbs can be used in diverse ways, which means that they are very flexible in sentences; they can be moved around quite a bit without causing any grammatical irregularities.

PLACEMENT OF ADVERBS

1. Adverbs used to begin sentences/clauses

Connecting adverbs: Consequently, However, Next, Still, Then, etc.

- I did not care for her tone. However, I let it go.
- That was the Medieval section of the museum; next, we have the Industrial Revolution.

Adverbs of time: Tomorrow, Yesterday, Sometimes, etc.

- Tomorrow, I am leaving for Calcutta.
- Sometimes, we feel as if we do not belong in this group.

2. Adverbs in the middle

Focusing adverbs:

- **Adverbs of frequency: often, rarely, never, always, etc.**
  You are always late.

- **Adverbs of certainty: perhaps, probably, certainly, maybe, etc.**
  I will probably be absent at the party.

- **Adverbs of comment: adverbs that are used to express opinion, such as smartly, responsibly, intelligently, etc.**
  He acted responsibly by informing the authorities about the wallet he had found.

3. Adverbs to end sentences

- **Adverbs of manner: used to describe how something is done**
  He wrote the answers correctly.

- **Adverbs of place: used to describe the place where an event occurs**
  Father is sleeping upstairs.

- **Adverbs of time: find their ways to the ends of sentences or clauses.**
  I leave tomorrow afternoon.

LIST OF ADVERBS:

1.	boldly	11.	gleefully	21.	powerfully	31.	boastfully
2.	bravely	12.	gracefully	22.	safely	32.	dejectedly
3.	brightly	13.	happily	23.	victoriously	33.	enviously
4.	cheerfully	14.	honestly	24.	warmly	34.	foolishly
5.	deftly	15.	innocently	25.	vivaciously	35.	hopelessly
6.	devotedly	16.	kindly	26.	achingly	36.	irritably
7.	eagerly	17.	merrily	27.	angrily	37.	jealously
8.	elegantly	18.	obediently	28.	annoyingly	38.	joylessly
9.	faithfully	19.	perfectly	29.	anxiously	39.	lazily
10.	fortunately	20.	politely	30.	badly	40.	miserably

EXERCISE 61

Q117] Circle the adverbs. Complete the sentences using the adverbs from the word bank.

[A] Word bank: early mouse always carefully soon helicopter quietly eventually bear near skillfully salmon bus privately normally

1. Karina _______ took the eggs out of the fridge.
2. Andrew and Tom _______________ painted the fence.
3. Mona arrived _______________ for her riding lesson.
4. This is a chat we need to have _______________.
5. They will _______________ finish reading this book.
6. She _______________ takes the attendance folder to the office.
7. Enzo _______________ gets to go with dad to the store!
8. Fred tiptoed _______________ up the stairs.
9. The movie I want to see is coming out _______________.
10. Place the flowers in the vase _______________ the window.

[B] Circle the adverbs.

happily   tomorrow   dinosaur   noisily   pretty   outside   quickly
cruelly   flowerpot   daily   always   uncle   badly   gladly   before

Complete the sentences using the adverbs from above.

1. We played _______________ because it was a nice day.
2. The bully treated us _______________.
3. My aunt leaves for China _______________.
4. The cats meowed _______________ for their dinner.
5. I read _______________ because I love to learn.
6. We _______________ went with our dad to get ice cream.
7. The boy who behaved _______________ got a time out.
8. I _______________ ate the last chocolate donut.
9. My brother ran _______________ to catch the bus.
10. Dogs _______________ love to eat a bone.

[C] Circle the adverbs.

Shyly   angrily   animal   inside   clearly   playfully   robot   calmly
bravely   quietly   circus   yearly   wildly   sternly   windy

Complete the sentences using the adverbs from above.

1. The kitten pawed the string _______________.
2. We whispered _______________ during the movie.
3. The principal talked to us _______________ when we were late.
4. My family travels to the lake _______________.
5. They walked _______________ into the haunted house.
6. When it is raining, we read comics _______________.
7. Monkeys act _______________ when they have bananas.
8. Jack sees _______________ when he wears his glasses.
9. Nina responded _______________ when her sister teased her.
10. They exited the school _______________ for the fire drill.

Q118] (A) Complete the story with either adjectives or adverbs. You can use the ones suggested or write your own.

Word bank: busy   greatly   adorable   active
small   happily   lovely   lazily   nosily   big   eagerly

Andy's _____________ cat, Lia, had kittens. They were _______________ little creatures that were starting to _____________ explore Andy's house. They _______________ hopped and ran all over the living room, chasing each other and trying _______________ to climb on the _______________ couch. Lia _______________ watch her _______________ babies as she laid on her bed in the corner of the _____________ room. Andy was _________________ following the _____________ kittens around hoping that they would play with him.

(B) Complete the story with either adjectives or adverbs. You can use the ones suggested or write your own.

Word bank: big   large   eventually   tired   finally
little   long   rigid   safely   small   stubborn   tirelessly

The _____________ mouse was ______________ trying to get a ___________ piece of cheese through a _____________ hole in the wall. The _____________ mouse pushed and pushed but could not make the _______________ piece of food fit in the _____________ hole. ___________ , the mouse ate a piece of the cheese hoping that the smaller piece would __________ fit in. It took a __________ time, but the shrinking cheese _____________ rolled through the hole and could be stored __________ in the mouse's pantry.

(C) Complete the story with either adjectives or adverbs. You can use the ones suggested or write your own.

Word bank: closely   huddled   cool   dark   finally   humorous
lazily   long   lovely   patiently   scary   squarely   big

It was a __________ summer night and the boy scouts were camping near the lake. They had built a __________ fire around which they sat

___________ to warm up. The night was ___________ but ___________ as the breeze ___________ blew around the camp. The troop leader seated ___________ on a tree log was telling ___________ stories and ___________ jokes. The children were listening ___________ , waiting ___________ for the end of the story to retreat in their tent and ___________ sleep. It had been a very ___________ day.

EXERCISE 62

HOW, WHEN & WHERE ADVERBS

Q119] Circle the verb the underlined adverb describes. Write if the adverb tells how, when or where the action happens.

[A] ___How___ 1. Ellie (punched) in the code <u>confidently</u>.

___________ 2. Felicia arrived <u>late</u> at the party.

___________ 3. Jamie lives <u>near</u> the park.

___________ 4.Kate finished her homework <u>earlier</u> than she planned.

___________ 5. Rob performed <u>remarkably</u> on stage.

___________ 6. The store seems <u>farther</u> than expected.

___________ 7. I hope the show starts <u>soon</u>.

___________ 8. <u>Hopefully</u>, they can come to the party.

___________ 9. Put the pot <u>here</u>, by the stove.

___________ 10. The man shook her hand <u>firmly</u>.

___________ 11. The dance will begin <u>later</u> than we thought.

___________ 12. We will walk <u>there</u> together.

[B] ___When___ 1. The practice began <u>sooner</u> than we thought.

___________ 2. The movie ended <u>later</u> than expected.

_____________ 3. This race began <u>earlier</u> than the last one.

_____________ 4. She is supposed to be here <u>now</u>.

_____________ 5. Be careful, there is juice <u>everywhere</u>.

_____________ 6. Hang your coat <u>there</u>, by the door.

_____________ 7. Come <u>here</u>, please.

_____________ 8. The Jones are moving <u>far</u> from here.

_____________ 9. She dances <u>gracefully</u>.

_____________ 10. The little boy answered the question <u>politely</u>.

_____________ 11. Finish this task <u>rapidly</u> so we can move to the next.

_____________ 12. You should always answer the phone <u>promptly</u>.

[C] __Where__ 1. The girl twirled all around.

_____________ 2. Drop the parcel here, thank you.

_____________ 3. The try-outs start tomorrow.

_____________ 4. He knew her before she became famous.

_____________ 5. Jamie wrote neatly on the board.

_____________ 6. The fisherman walked slowly on the frozen lake.

_____________ 7. Place the propane tank farther from the house.

_____________ 8. I was sure the grocery store was nearby.

_____________ 9. You missed the time; the boys played yesterday.

_____________ 10. I wished the game started later.

_____________ 11. Maggie plays the trombone louder than Irene.

_____________ 12. I honestly do not know the answer.

EXERCISE 63

Q120] (A) Circle the adverbs.

Word bank: drink equally finally gallon gently here ignore later legally locally monster nervously party telepathically telephone thoroughly today union vision yesterday

(B) Complete the sentences using the adverbs from above.

1.   The report on pollution comes out _____today_____.
2.   ____________, we are doing everything by the book.
3.   The twins communicate ____________ with one another.
4.   Our favorite team won the championship ____________.
5.   Leave your shoes ____________. You don't need to wear them in the house.
6.   Grandma ____________ finished the quilt she promised me.
7.   The skaters were ____________ awaiting the results of the competition.
8.   The pie was shared ____________ among the children.
9.   The teacher explained the problem ____________.
10. Your parents will arrive ____________ this afternoon.
11. The woman placed her infant ________ in his crib.
12. These vegetables are grown ____________.

Q121] (A) Circle the adverbs.

weakly greatly building daily ladder shiny poorly suddenly clumsily bashfully excitedly instantly dragon later outdoors never strictly chopped generously raced

(B) Complete the sentences using the adverbs from above.

1.   Rachel buys a candy ________ to satisfy her sweet tooth.
2.   I will play with you ____________ because I am busy now.
3.   The principal ____________ enforced the school rules.
4.   My uncle ________ gave me his old baseball card collection.

5. We eat ______________ in the summer when it is not raining.
6. Ted __________ limped across the finish line.
7. I responded ___________ when my sister cried for help.
8. Sue ________ eats peanuts because she is allergic to them.
9. I __________ opened all of my birthday presents.
10. The alarm rang ___________ and startled all of us.
11. Jeff __________ tripped over his dog and scraped his knee.
12. We _______ appreciated all of the help our teacher gave us.

Q122] (A) Circle the adverbs.

urgently   wrap   truly   often   salty   today   sparingly   loyally
bulldozer   carefully   cellphone   softly   densely   turkey   prickly
after   busily   green   equally   hourly

(B) Complete the sentences using the adverbs from above.

1. My dad checks his email ______________.
2. Tommy ________________ plays with his toy trucks.
3. I went to the doctor for my sports physical ______________.
4. She uses the pepper ______________ because it is spicy.
5. We ________________ play kickball during recess at school.
6. The forest is ________________ populated with trees.
7. I sang ______________ to my baby sister to help her sleep.
8. They skated ________________ on the frozen pond.
9. We saw a movie and left immediately ___________.
10. My mom loves all of her children ________________.
11. Abby __________ called for her dad when she got a splinter.
12. Steve ______________ watches every game his team plays.

EXERCISE 64

RELATIVE ADVERB: WHERE, WHY AND WHEN

Where expresses a place.

Why expresses a reason.

When expresses a time.

Q123] Fill in the blank with the correct word: where, why, or when.

(A)

1. Do you know _______the pencils are in the classroom?
2. _______________ are we learning chemistry in the fourth grade?
3. She will go to the store _______________ she is on her way to work.
4. I asked my dad _______________ we are going to visit grandma.
5. This is the place _______________ we first met.
6. _______________ did you live when you were five years old?
7. I never knew _______________ he was so mad at me.
8. _______________ does the next train leave the station?
9. I used to play soccer _______________ I was little.
10. My mom works in an office _______________ Jaden's mom also works.
11. _______________ didn't you wear a coat today in the snow?
12. I wonder _______________ I left my coffee mug.

(B)

1. Did you see <u>where</u> the truck went?
2. _______________ is Toby going on vacation?
3. Meredith wonders _______________ she will need to get a haircut.
4. He has no idea _______________ he is driving.
5. _______________ is the party this Friday night?
6. She didn't understand _______________ her car wouldn't start.
7. _______________ is your birthday?
8. Let's meet _______________ we are done with our homework.
9. I saw the man standing _______________ we had parked our bikes.
10. I wonder _______________ we didn't pack any food for the picnic.
11. This is not the place_______________ I go to school.
12. _______________ does the girl ride a horse to her grandma's house?

(C)

1.   <u>When</u> did you make this delicious cake?
2.   My family drinks hot cocoa _______________ it snows.
3.   I didn't see _______________ my dog went.
4.   _______________ did your friend buy his new shoes?
5.   I wasn't sure _______________ the doctor said to eat an apple a day.
6.   This is the day _______________ my little sister was born.
7.   Darren was in the room _______________ the blue chair was.
8.   He asked the teacher _______________ he had to wear a purple shirt on Friday.
9.   Did anyone see _______________ my paper airplane landed?
10. _______________ is Thanksgiving always on a Thursday?
11. He will buy a house _______________ he has enough money.
12. _______________ are we going to eat dinner?

EXERCISE 65

ADVERB PHRASES

Adverb phrases usually describe when, where or how something happens.

He ran by the lake.

The adverb phrase "by the lake" describes where he ran.

Q124] Improve the following sentences by adding an adverbial phrase from the word bank.

[A] Word bank: After the meeting, For many years, In the yard, Near my house, Without any help

1.   _______________ he completed his project.
2.   _______________ she prepared for the party.
3.   _______________ we found a baby frog.
4.   _______________ there were a lot of cars.
5.   _______________ my parents never asked me about my grades.

[B] Word bank: Over the hill, Inside the room, Without looking, Near the creek, From the balcony

1. __________________ he could see the ocean.
2. __________________ she saw a coyote that was heading her way.
3. __________________ they started to cross the street.
4. __________________ there were no windows.
5. __________________ frogs make all sorts of noise.

[C] Word bank: In the classroom, After many hours, Outside the school, With a lot of energy, Far from the river

1. __________________ she waited for her friends.
2. __________________ he ran to the finish line.
3. __________________ the family went hiking.
4. __________________ they sang the song.
5. __________________ we could not find the solution to the problem.

11

PREPOSITIONS

Prepositions are the words which are used to connect the different nouns, pronouns, and phrases in a sentence. It functions to introduce or precede the word or phrase to be connected, called the object of the preposition.

The preposition usually indicates the relation between the words it is connecting. It tells whether the words are connected in actual space or a place, or related through time or are they part of a thought or process.

Prepositional phrases are the preposition and its object and any adjectives or adverbs that were applied to the object. The prepositional phrase as a whole can also be used as a noun, adverb or adjective.

Example: *He found the book **on** the table.*

- Here the preposition is **'on'** as it shows the relation in place between the book and the table.
- The prepositional phrase is '**on** the table' which is acting as an Adverb telling where the book was found.

Example: *She went **to** sleep early.*

- In this sentence the preposition is **'to'** which is introducing where or in what state had the noun gone into.

Example: *Her house was **beside** a steep hill.*

- The preposition here is **beside** which is telling the place where the house was.
- The prepositional phrase is 'beside a steep hill' which is acting as an adverb.

Types of Prepositions

Simple Prepositions

These prepositions are constructed by only one word like: **On, at, about, with, after, for,** etc.

Example: *He found the book **about** dogs **on** the table, **in** the bedroom.*

Here is a list of common simple prepositions (preposition examples):

For, By, At, On, Of, Off, To

Double Prepositions

These prepositions are formed by combining two words or two Simple Prepositions: **Into, within, upon, onto,** etc.

Example: *The dog jumped **onto** the bed and left marks **upon** the sheets.*

Here is a list of common double prepositions (preposition examples):

Into, Onto, Upto, From Behind, From Beneath, Out Of, Upon

Compound Prepositions

These prepositions are two-word prepositions.

According to, because of, next to, due to, etc.

Example: *He was upset **because of** his son's behaviour.*

Here is a list of common compound prepositions (preposition examples):

Across, Along, Beside, Behind, Before, Without, Inside

Participle Prepositions

Participles are actually verbs that end with '-en' or '-ing'. As these verbs were commonly and very popularly used as prepositions by the people, these verbs have been given special status as prepositions.

Considering, during, given, including, etc.

Example: ***Considering*** *what he had **to** work with, he did a pretty good job.*

Here is a list of common participle prepositions (preposition examples):

Concerning, Pending, During, Given, Failing, Excluding, Phrase, Prepositions

These prepositions are a combination of **the preposition + a modifier (optional) + the object.** They are used to modify the nouns, verbs or sentences and also complete clauses.

At home, in time, with me, from my father, under the blanket, etc.

Example: The clothes left **on the bed** have been ironed and kept back.

Here is a list of common phrase prepositions (preposition examples):

At high speed, By all means, For a change, In accordance with, On a journey, Out of curiosity, To the best of

Prepositions can only be learnt by memory; unfortunately, there is no method or particular way to recognize and learn them.

List of Prepositions

These classifications above are based on the construction of the prepositions themselves. Apart from this, prepositions are also categorized based on their use in a sentence as:

- Prepositions of place.
- Prepositions of time.
- Prepositions of movement.

Prepositions of Place

What are <u>prepositions of place</u>?

Prepositions of place refer to those prepositions that can be used to show where something is located. There are three basic prepositions of place: in, on, at.

For example:

At college, At home, At reception, In a taxi, In the sky, In the building, On the way, On the radio, On the page,

Prepositions of Time

What are <u>prepositions of time</u>?

The prepositions are often used to refer to times and dates. There are three basic prepositions of time: at, in, on

- 'At' is used for precise times.
- 'In' is used for months, years, decades, centuries and long periods of time.
- 'On' is used for days and dates.

For examples:

- At 10.30am, At 8 o'clock, At bedtime, At breakfast, In 16 year's time, In 1991., In December, On Christmas, On Friday, On holiday

Prepositions of Movement

What are <u>prepositions of movement</u>?

Prepositions of movement show movement from one place to another. There are 9 basic prepositions that pertain to movement: To, Towards, Through, Into, Across, Over, Along, In, On

Uses:

To- used when there is a specific destination in mind.

Towards- movement in the direction of something.

Through- movement across something, i.e. from one side of it to the other.

Across- movement from one end of something to the other.

Over- describe something's position when it is above something else.

Along- movement in a line.

In- something's position in relation to the area or space or place surrounding it.

On- describe something's position in relation to a surface.

Into- movement causing something to hit something else.

For example:

- *Can you direct me to the nearest post office?*
- *He was walking menacingly towards me.*
- *The train went through the tunnel.*
- *He walked across the road.*

<u>**EXERCISE 66**</u>

IDENTIFYING PREPOSITIONS

Prepositions are words which often **tell us where or when something is.** Common prepositions include *at, above, before, to, in, from, beside, between, by* and *about.*

Q125] Circle the preposition in each sentence.

(A) 1. We played in the park.

2)   My family went to Florida.

3)   My mom works with your mom.

4)   The dogs dove in the pool.

5)   Can you go with me?

6)   The bus comes from the school.

7)   The doctor buys candy for his patients.

8)   The chair is by the back door.

9)   I left my backpack on the floor.

10) She drank a glass of water.

11) We picked the flowers off the ground.

12) The gift was from my mom.

(B) 1. My family went to the store.

2)   Michael came from Georgia.

3)   We were in the pool.

4)   My parents traveled out of town.

5)   The boys put their gloves on the ground.

6)   We got off the train.

7)   This is a cake for the students.

8)   The house was full of spiders.

9)   He left his coat by his shoes.

10) Can we go with my friends?

11) Are we heading to New York?

12) My brother bought some flowers for his girlfriend.

(C) 1 I would like a piece of pizza.

2) Ryan was in Colombo.

3) We walked off the path.

4) I got a new bike from my dad.

5) We went out the door.

6) We should go to your house.

7) Did you find my note on the table?

8) We ordered a pizza for the team.

9) Can we just leave our shoes by the door?

10) I love going to the museum.

11) We get on the bus every morning.

12) I'm making a necklace for my mom.

<u>EXERCISE 67</u>

Prepositions connect words to more information about place, time, or direction.

Q126] Fill in the blanks using prepositions from the word bank.

[By from to with in of for out on off]

(A) 1. I went ____the store _____my family.

2. Can you buy me a gift ________ my birthday please?

3. We have always lived ________ a lot of pets.

4. My mom was mad because I left all _____ my clothes ______ the floor.

5. Did you want to stop ______ Tennessee when we drive _____ Florida?

6. My grandma is originally ________Russia.

7. I like to spend time ________ my room.

8. We got a new car __________ my big brother.

9. My family went __________ the door.

10. Bruce went _______France _________ his vacation _______his friends.

(B) 1. He received a package <u>from</u> his best friend.

2. The scout leader told us not to walk __________ the marked path.

3. My favorite spot is __________ the park __________ the pond.

4. Did you go __________ the beautiful, sandy beaches?

5. I had to visit __________ my mom and dad.

6. She wanted a slice __________ ham and a coffee.

7. My brother is having a party __________ his sixteenth birthday.

8. Her family is planning to go __________ Florida __________ December.

9. Can you leave your keys __________ the table so I can find them?

10. I dance often __________ my best friend, Stacy.

(C) 1. My parents went <u>off</u> the road <u>in</u> their new car.

2. The cat ran __________ the door.

3. Did you see the alligator __________ the water's edge?

4. I am going __________ the dance __________ my best friend, Tony.

5. I got the most amazing gift __________ my grandma.

6. Could you please cut me a piece __________ pie?

7. This is the blanket I made __________ the new baby.

8. It is not polite to leave your dirty dishes __________ the table.

9. Serena and Kia are going __________ Indiana __________ a party.

10. My mom didn't want to see the movie ________ my dad.

EXERCISE 68

PREPOSITIONAL PHRASES

Prepositions + objects = prepositional phrases

Prepositional phrases (*at home, across the street*) **always begin with a preposition** and include the object of the preposition, usually a noun or pronoun. A prepositional phrase gives us information about place, time or direction.

Q127] (A) Rewrite the sentence adding a prepositional phrase from the list.

Prepositional phrases: on Friday, with her parents, in the park, to the game, for her birthday

1. She wants to visit her friend. _________________________________
2. There is a party. _________________________________
3. Did you see the dog? ______________________________
4. He will drive. _____________________________
5. They ran. ___________________________

(B) Write sentences using these prepositional phrases:

1. over the bridge ______________________________
2. through the door ______________________________
3. inside the house ______________________________
4. to the museum ______________________________
5. with the cat ______________________________

Q128] (A) Rewrite the sentence adding a prepositional phrase from the list.

Prepositional phrases: in my room, with my teachers, to the left, around the yard, under my bed

1. I hide my secret journals. _______________________________________
2. My parents won't let me have a television. _______________________
3. Theprincipalsarehavingameeting._________________________________
4. My dog loves to run. ____
5. We need to turn the car. ____

(B) Write sentences using these prepositional phrases:

1. down the stairs ____
2. from my grandparents ____
3. by the fireplace ____
4. to school ____
5. with the entire family ____

EXERCISE 69

Q129] Choose the correct prepositions.

(i)   What are you doing ______________ the weekend?
(ii)   I don't know yet. Maybe I'll go to the cinema ______________ saturday.
(iii) That's interesting. I haven't been to the cinema ______________ so many years.
(iv)   We could go there together ______________ the afternoon.
(v)   That would be great. But I would prefer to go there______________ the evening. I am visiting my grandma ______________ Saturday
(vi)   That's okay. The films starts ______________ eight o'clock.
(vii) I can pick you up half ______________ seven. How long does the film last?
(viii) It lasts ______________ two hours and forty-five minutes
(ix)   ______________ two hours and forty-five minutes.
(x)   ______________ eight ______________ a quarter ______________ eleven.
(xi)   That's right. But I must hurry home ______________ the film. I have to be home ______________ eleven o'clock.

Q130] Complete the sentences by adding prepositions.

   (i)   The first Mc Donald's restaurant was opened ______________ Dick and Mac McDonald the 15th ______________ May 1940.

   (ii)   The best selling products ______________ their restaurant were humburgers.

   (iii)   So the McDonald brothers thought ______________ a way to produce humburgers more quickly.

   (iv)   This was introduced ______________ 1948 and became known ______________ the Speedy Service System.

   (v)   The first franchised McDonald's restaurant was opened ______________ 1953, and today you can find Mcdonald's restaurants ______________ more than 100 countries.

   (vi)   The meats ______________ the burgers vary ______________ the culture ______________ the country.

   (vii)   Franchisees and future managers ______________ McDonald's restaurants are trained Humburger University, which is.located ______________ Oak Brook, a suburb ______________ Chicago.

   (viii)   McDonalds is also known ______________ its sponsorship ______________ various international sport events.

Q131] Complete the exercise according to the picture.

   (i)   ______________ the picture, I can see a woman.

   (ii)   The woman is sitting ______________ a chair.

   (iii)   She is sitting ______________ a chair.

   (iv)   There is another chair ______________ the woman.

   (v)   Her feet are ______________ the table.

   (vi)   The woman is holding a cup ______________ her hands.

   (vii)   ______________ the table are a laptop, a paper, a calculator, an appointment calendar, two pens and a muffin.

   (viii)   The woman's looking ______________ her laptop

   (ix)   The woman's bag is ______________ the table.

Q132] Fill in the blanks with appropriate prepositions:

1. Diwali is .... 10 November.
2. Gandhiji lived .... the English rule.
3. They finished work .... sunset.
4. Gandhiji was born .... 1869 and died .... 30 January, 1948.
5. I will call at your house sometime .... he evening.
6. Shankar's birthday is .... 3 March.
7. The train leaves Delhi .... 3.00 pm and reaches Chandigarh .... 7.00 pm.
8. He should be here .... now.
9. Please come to my office at 11.00 am .... Tuesday afternoon.
10. Pramod will see you .... Monday .... 11.00 am.

<u>EXERCISE 70</u>

Q133] Fill in the blanks with prepositions in the following sentences:

1. You must reach there .... week-end.
2. The robbers entered the house .... the night.
3. The exhibition will be opened .... 10 am .... Friday.
4. The interested candidates should report for interview latest .... 3 June 2007.

5. He came to my house ……… my absence.
6. The examinations will commence ……….. April 1 ……….. 9.00 am.
7. Send your reply ……. March 3, the latest.
8. We are having a variety show ………… Saturday.
9. Are you coming to see us ………. Diwali ?
10. A gale got up ………… night and did much damage.

Q134] Supply the correct preposition in the following:

1. Does he live ……….. the town, or ……….. the country ?
2. Have you lived …………… Kharkhoda long ?
3. I have always wanted to live ……….. a bungalow.
4. Mr. Sharma lives ………….. Model Town ………….. Delhi.
5. He lives …………… 194 Kali Bari Kolkata.
6. My father works …………. an office.
7. My uncle lives ………….. a mansion ……………... a village a few miles from Mumbai.
8. James was brought up …………. a farm but at the age of 11 he was sent to work a small town.
9. His father is the manager ……………... the local bank.
10. How long have you been …………. Delhi ?

Q135] Fill in the blanks with proper prepositions:

besides, between, among, since, for, by, with.

1. He was standing ………….. her.
2. I write …………. a pen.
3. I have not seen him …………. he left for England.
4. It has been raining hard ………… the last 3 days.
5. India beat Bangladesh …………. an innings.
6. Distribute the fruit ………. the students.
7. The two friends will settle it …………. them.
8. ……….. being a teacher, he is also a poet.

Q136] Fill in the blanks in the following sentences using one of the options from the brackets:

1. There is a cow (on/at/in/of) the field.
2. He is fond (on/at/in/of) tea.
3. The cat jumped (on/at/in/of) the chair.
4. What are you looking (on/at/in/of) ?
5. It is true according (with/by/for/to) law.
6. A man is known (with/by/for/to) the company he keeps.
7. I do not agree (with/by/for/to) you.
8. What are you looking (with/by/for/to) ?
9. Let us move (by/with/for/on).
10. The book lies (on/at/for/of) the table.

Q137] Fill in the blanks with appropriate prepositions.

1. The working hours will be less tomorrow………….Diwali.
2. The customer care can be contacted…………. any queries.
3. She stopped talking………. and then began to laugh.
4. Cargo ship sank……….. of Ukraine.
5. You can make the arrangements for the event
6. You can wear blue…………
7. We have been travelling for a long time…………. the treasure.
8. The villagers are ……….. warm clothes during winters.
9. As a young man he travelled a lot and was always
10. We have brought home somebody else's luggage ……….. yours.

12

CONJUNCTIONS

A conjunction is a word which connects two words or clauses or sentences and shows the relation between them. They are used to avoid making the text seem like bullet points and to make the text flow. For examples:

- *Jai saw a dog on the road. He decided to adopt the dog. Jai brought the dog home.*
- *Jai saw a dog on the road **and** decided to adopt the dog, **so** he brought the dog home.*

Here '**and**' and '**so**' are conjunctions which are used to join the sentences and show the relation between them.

<u>Types of Conjunctions</u>

There are three main categories of conjunctions that are explained below.

Coordinating Conjunctions

These conjunctions are used to link or join two words or phrases that are equally important and complete in terms of grammar when compared with each other. The sentences or words do not depend on anything to give themselves meaning.

Coordinating Conjunctions Examples:

There are seven main coordinating conjunctions: For, And, Nor, But, Or, Yet, Soon

For examples:

- *I told her to leave, **for** I was very tired.*
- *The bowl of squid eyeball stew is hot **and** delicious.*
- *We can neither change **nor** improve it.*
- *You may delay, **but** time will not.*
- *There were ten **or** twelve people in the room.*
- *Her advice seems strange, **yet** I believe she's right.*
- *As you make your bed, **so** you must lie upon it.*

Subordinating Conjunctions

These conjunctions are used to join an independent and complete clause with a dependent clause that relies on the main clause for meaning and relevance.

The dependent clause cannot exist on its own as a sentence and often does not make sense without the main clause.

It comes before the dependent clause but the dependent clause itself can be placed either ahead of or following the independent clause.

List of Subordinating conjunctions: Although, As, After, as soon as, because, by the time, even though, if, in case, now that, before, once, though, until, whether, etc.

For examples:

*I have great/the greatest respect for his ideas, **although** I don't agree with them.*

- *The lion is not so <u>fierce</u> **as** he is painted.*
- *Don't cry out **before** you are hurt.*
- ***Once** I've found somewhere to live I'll send you my address.*
- *They're coming next week, **though** I don't know which day.*
- *We didn't eat till past midnight.*

Correlative Conjunctions

Correlative Conjunctions are simply pairs of conjunctions used in a sentence to join different words or groups of words in a sentence together.

They are generally not used to link sentences, instead, they link two or more words of equal importance within the sentence itself.

Some of the more commonly used correlative conjunctions are: Both/and; Either/or; If/then; Rather/than; Just as/so; Neither/nor; Not only/but also; Whether/or; Hardly/when; No sooner/than, etc.

For examples:

- ***Both*** *the shoes **and** the dress were completely overpriced.*
- ***Either*** *her parents **or** she is invited to the party tonight.*
- ***Neither*** *I **nor** you are right.*
- *She is **not only** beautiful **but also** intelligent.*
- *We can't decide **whether** to paint the wall red **or** white.*
- *I **hardly** had time to ring the bell **before** the door opened.*

EXERCISE 71

AND, BUT OR SO

Q138] Complete the text with and, but, or so.

(A) The Picnic

Today was the day! Mary's family were going on a picnic. Mother prepared sandwiches _______ drinks that father placed in a basket. Everyone was ready, _________ they left the house. They walked together to the park. Arrived at the perfect spot, dad unfolded a blanket _________ mom set the basket down. Mary _________ her sister were excited, _________ they kept jumping on the blanket until mom told them to stop. Before long, everyone was sitting down, _________ mom was opening the basket. She handed each one a sandwich _________ a napkin. She looked for the drinks _________ could not find them. It seems that dad had forgotten to pack them. Thankfully, there was a fountain in the park __________ everyone could drink some water. After the picnic, they packed everything __________ returned home. Everyone laughed when they saw the four drinks still on the counter.

(B) Grandma's Rocking Chair

We were visiting my grandma when she told my dad that her rocking chair was broken. Dad looked at it __but__ could not fix it there, __________ we took it home with us. That night, dad asked me to help fix grandma's rocking chair. We brought it to the garage __________ dad set it on the floor. He looked at it __________ asked me for a screwdriver. I went to the toolbox __________ found several. I brought two back __________ asked my dad if he wanted the red one __________ the blue one. He took the red one. Then, he asked me to hold the chair steady __________ he could replace a fallen screw. After that, dad thought he was done, __________ the chair was still not working well. It turns out that the missing screw had fallen in the rocking mechanism __________ was stopping the chair from going. Dad got some pliers __________ took it out. Now grandma's chair was fixed!

(C) The Gift

It was Mark's birthday __and__ his dad came home with a special gift. Mark was excited to know what was in it, __________ he quickly opened the box. Inside, he found a cute, fluffy, __________ orange kitten looking up at him. Mark took him out of the box, __________ he was not sure how to hold it. Quickly, the kitten left his hand __________ climbed up his sleeve. Mark wrapped his arms around it, __________ it would not fall, __________ the kitten continued to climb until it reached Mark's shoulder. There, it sat down __________ cuddled against Mark's neck. Mark did not know if he should leave it there __________ take it down, __________ before he could decide, the kitten began to purr. That is when Mark realized he had made a brand, new friend!

EXERCISE 72

Q139] Circle the conjunctions in each sentence.

A conjunction is a word that links two words or phrases together.

Common conjunctions: and, or, but, so, yet.

(A)

1. Supper was ready, but the children were not home. 2. She likes chocolate pudding, lemon meringue pie, and black forest cake. 3. Do you want to sit in the chair or on the sofa? 4. We waited, but the bus never came. 5. I will be quiet, so you can finish your homework. 6. The little girl was tired, yet she did not want to go to bed. 7. John stayed inside at recess, so he could work on his project. 8. The soup tastes good, but it could be warmer. 9. Gerry plays hockey in the winter and soccer in the summer. 10. It was raining, so we took the bus home. 11. Finish your vegetables, or you will not have dessert. 12. He knew the answer, but he was too shy to raise his hand.

(B)

1. The bus was full, so they walked home. 2. She enjoyed the cake, but she refused a second piece. 3. May you share the salt and pepper please? 4. I'll have the white sugar, and you can have the brown sugar. 5. Do you prefer apple or orange juice? 6. Time was up, yet I was not finished. 7. The boy was tired, but he kept running. 8. You cannot go to school or to the playground when you are sick. 9. The restaurant was closed, yet the lights were on. 10. I will hang my clothes, so they will dry. 11. John was asleep, but his brother was still awake. 12. You can walk, run or take the bus.

(C)

1. He took swimming lessons, so he is no longer afraid of the water. 2. The cake has ready, but we weren't allowed to eat it. 3. On our trip we will ski, surf and golf. 4. Our Dad asked us if we wanted to ski, surf or golf today. 5. Mary wants to play with Audra, but she must finish her homework. 6. You can color the sun orange or yellow. 7. Jeremy like nachos and salsa. 8. She said she called, yet the phone never rang. 9. The drive-in movie will start soon, so we should stop talking. 10. Put the leftover food in the fridge, or the dog will eat it. 11. The ball game was over, so the players shook hands. 12. My shoes, pants and coat all get wet when it rains or snows.

<u>EXERCISE 73</u>

CONNECTING WORDS WITH CONJUNCTIONS

Q140] Combine the two sentences using the word in brackets.

Conjunctions link two words, phrases or clauses.

Paul likes apples. Paul likes oranges. (and)

Paul likes apples and oranges.

(A) 1.Nathan likes chocolate. He likes ice cream. (and)

____

2. The girls went to the mall. They went to the store. (and)

____

3. We could play Monopoly. We could play cards. (or)

____

4. My teacher is strict. He is fair. (but)

____

5. Mom asked my sister and me to clean our room. She asked us to vacuum. (and)

____

6. Do you want salad with your meat? Do you want rice? (or)

____

(B) 1. The painters finished the living room. They finished the kitchen. (and)

____

2. Leila plays with dolls. Leila plays with toy cars. (and)

____

3. You could finish your work. You could play outside. (or)

____

4. Jenna likes hot chocolate. She does not like coffee. (but)

____

5. The twins visited their grandparents. They went to a restaurant. (and)

____

6. You can have the blue marker. You can have the red marker. (or)

____

(C) 1. James hit his foot. He hit his toe. (and)

____

2. We can make spaghetti. We can make lasagna. (or)

____

3. We can read. We cannot talk. (but)

____

4. John wanted to go to the movie. He wanted to eat popcorn.(and)

____

5. They could bring dessert. They could bring salad. (or)

____

6. Ellie brushed her teeth. She combed her hair. (and)

____

EXERCISE 74

CONJUNCTIONS: CONNECTING MAIN CLAUSES

Q141] Use conjunctions & a comma to join sentences.

Do you want dessert? Would you prefer to go outside now? (or)

Do you want dessert, <u>or</u> would you prefer to go outside now?

(A) 1. Randy needs a haircut. He does not have any money. (but)

____

2. Joey emptied the litter box. He also gave the cat a bath. (and)

____

3. You could put your hair up in a bun. You could tie it in pigtails. (or)

____

4. Next summer, we could visit Florida. We could go to the Grand Canyon. (or)

____

5. Melanie bought cookies at the store. She put them away in the cupboard. (and)

____

6. My uncle would like to fly planes. He is afraid of heights. (but)

____

(B) 1. We could walk to the park. We could go swimming. (or)

____

2. Fanny enjoys baking. There is no flour left. (but)

____

3. They play with trucks. They put their toys away. (and)

____

4. Linda wrote her name on the sheet. She answered the first question. (and)

____

5. Jeremy wanted to play baseball. It started raining. (but)

____

6. Do you want waffles? Do you prefer pancakes? (or)

____

(C) 1. We will go to the store. We will put gas in the car. (and)

____

2. We should make some popcorn. We should watch a movie. (and)

____

3. Dad would like another piece of cake. He is still full from supper. (but)

____

4. I would help you thread this needle. I do not have my glasses. (but)

____

5. Do you want to have a shower? Do you prefer to take a bath? (or)

____

6. We could start with a salad. We could start with soup. (or)

____

<u>EXERCISE 75</u>

Coordinating conjunctions combine two independent clauses using a comma. for, and, nor, but, or, yet, so

Q142] Combine the two sentences into one sentence by adding a coordinating conjunction and a comma.

(A) 1. We are going to the store now. You won't have to go later.

____

2. I thought I had won the race. I really came in second place.

____

3. My family is going on vacation. We are going to visit my grandma.

____

4. We can either eat spaghetti for dinner. We can eat at the local pizza place.

____

5. He didn't go to the wedding. He still sent the bride and groom a present.

____

6. They had a lot of money. They had inherited millions from their grandparents.

____

7. I tried the new dessert. I really didn't like the way it tasted.

____

8. The computer is either broken. The computer needs to be turned on.

____

(B) 1. I have to stay here. I really don't want to.

____

2. We bought the bread. We forgot to buy any drinks for the picnic.

____

3. Pam is always laughing. She finds everything hilarious.

____

4. The worker lives two minutes from the hotel. She always walks to work.

____

5. Tony plans to move to California. He will attend college there.

____

6. The boys lost the game. They all had a really great time.

____

7. It is time to go to school. We are about to miss the bus.

___

8. I wanted to see the painting. I never went to the museum.

___

(C) 1. People love to cook. They don't like to do the dishes after.

___

2. My mom loves flowers. We are going to get her some for her birthday.

___

3. My friend, Jim is great to be with. He is fun and kind.

___

4. We made a giant cake. It was delicious.

___

5. Either we can go to the park. We can visit the ice cream shop.

___

6. Scott dances at a studio. He does a fantastic job at his competitions.

___

7. My family wanted to buy a new car. We got a new dog instead.

___

8. I want to be a doctor. I don't want to go to college.

___

EXERCISE 76

SUBORDINATING CONJUNCTIONS

Subordinating conjunctions are used to **create complex sentences out of a main clause and a dependent clause**.

Note: Students should notice that commas are only used between the clauses when the conjunction is at the start of the sentence.

Q143] Complete the sentences with a conjunction from the word bank.

(A) Word bank: although, because, before, If, once, since, unless, whenever, while

1. ___Before___ you go to bed, brush your teeth.
2. Brush your teeth ____________ you go to bed.
3. It is cold outside ____________ it is already summer.
4. You do not need to help me ____________ you want to.
5. You can come to our house ____________ you are in the neighborhood.
6. ____________ it is late, you can have a glass of milk.
7. Set the table ____________ I make supper.
8. I will wash the dishes ____________ you finish your plate.
9. ____________ you start working on your homework, I will come and help you.

(B) Word bank: after, because, before, even, though, once, since, until, when, while

1. We need to cut the apples ________ we make the pie.
2. ____________ we make the pie, we need to cut the apples.
3. ____________ you are ready, we should go.
4. She watched the scary movie ____________ she was scared.
5. We missed the first part of the movie ____________ we were late.
6. ____________ the grass is cut, we can play croquet.

7.   You should drink your tea ______________ the water is hot.

8.   ______________ you are the boss, you can listen to people.

9.   It has to get very cold ______________ the pond freezes.

10.   ______________ the pond freezes, it has to get very cold.

(C) Word bank: after, although, before, if, once, so, that, though, when, wherever

1.   __After__ your shower, dry your hair.

2.   Dry your hair ______________ you shower.

3.   ______________ you eat sugar, you get too noisy.

4.   Check both sides ______________ you cross the street.

5.   ______________ the sun is shining, it is still cold outside.

6.   ______________ he finished the race, his mother ran to him.

7.   Put the butter ______________ you find a spot.

8.   ______________ the floor is dry, you can walk on it.

9.   ______________ the parents are away, the kids play.

10.   The kids play ______________ the parents are away.

<u>EXERCISE 77</u>

Q144] Combine each pair of sentences using a conjunction from the word bank.

Conjunctions: after before although whenever while even though since until where when that because

(A) 1. The teacher let us listen to music. We worked on our papers.

____

2. I cannot find a good restaurant. I can eat for a good price.

____

3. She can visit her grandma. Her family travels to Florida this summer.

____

4. Michael wants to go to school. He can find a good job.

____

5. It is crazy. We have three tests on Friday.

____

(B) 1. We will eat dinner. We arrive at the restaurant.

____

2. He was carefully painting the room. We owned the house.

____

3. I love the house. I wish it were closer to my school.

____

4. She was singing a song. She was skipping to the park.

____

5. They will buy a new house. They win the big prize.

____

(C) 1. Shivansh plays pool. His brother prefers to play basketball.

____

2. I love to swim. We go to my uncle's pool.

____

3. Angela will bring us a cake. Her oven is broken.

____

4. This is the market. We buy all of our apples.

____

5. I keep my boots in my closet. Winter is over.

____

Q145] Combine each pair of sentences by using a subordinating conjunction at the start of the new sentence.

1. We are going to work faster. We don't need to be done until Saturday.

____

2. There is a lot to do. I leave for my vacation.

____

3. My brother wants to go to the lake. He loves to swim.

____

4. She drove the car. Mom was away.

____

5. Jill came tumbling. Jack had fallen.

____

6. My mom was watching her favorite show. She was cooking dinner.

____

7. My dad has worked at his company. I was born.

____

8. The coach wants us there. The game starts.

____

9. The teacher grades our papers. We take the test.

____

<u>EXERCISE 78</u>

COORDINATING AND SUBORDINATING CONJUNCTIONS

Coordinating conjunctions (for, and, nor, but, or, yet, so) combine two independent clauses using a comma.

Two sentences can also be combined by using a subordinating conjunction such as after, before, once, although, as if, as, because.

Q146] Circle the conjunction in each sentence. Write coordinating or subordinating to indicate the type of conjunction.

(A)

__subordinating__ 1. The chair is broken, so we tried to fix it.

_______________ 2. We have a lot to do, and no one wants to do any work.

_______________ 3. The car works after you put gasoline in it.

_______________ 4. The sandwich is delicious, so I'm buying another one.

_______________ 5. I am calling you because I need to talk to you about a problem.

_______________ 6. You can return the coat if it doesn't fit you well.

_______________ 7. Owen has a lot of friends, for he is kind and outgoing.

_______________ 8. The dog drinks water while he waits for his owner to walk him.

_______________ 9. The principal loves to go to school, but he doesn't like to work there on the weekends.

_______________ 10.Once we get to California, we will go to the beach.

_______________ 11. We lost the game, but we had a great time playing with our friends.

_______________ 12. The shirt was white, yet it looked yellow in the sunlight.

(B)

___________ 1. Before you go to bed, you need to take a shower.

___________ 2. I can find you wherever you go.

___________ 3. My grandma eats cake after she eats dinner every night.

___________ 4. We can talk about your grades, and we can look at different ways to study.

___________ 5. We were looking at the television when we saw a random light flashing in the kitchen.

___________ 6. Martin wanted to become a dentist, but he didn't want to go to school for a long time.

___________ 7. She is a really smart student, yet she doesn't do any homework.

___________ 8. He likes to go to the park because he likes to feed the ducks.

___________ 9. We will spend the day at the zoo unless it rains on Friday.

___________ 10. The teams will either play two games on Friday, or they will play two games on Saturday.

___________ 11. Now that we have limited space on the bus, each person can bring only one bag.

___________ 12. You can have your cell phone once you finish doing your chores.

(C)

<u>Subordinating</u>   1. This is the street where my parents met.

________________ 2. This jacket is big, so I will return it to the store.

________________ 3. I am running around the track until my mom shows up.

________________ 4. Since she was a little girl, my mom has loved knitting.

________________ 5. Robert is going to the concert, and he is bringing three friends.

________________ 6. We could go to the beach, but it is supposed to rain today.

________________ 7. Susan wanted to win the contest, so she studied every day during recess.

________________ 8. It is unusual that Martin didn't want to play the game.

________________ 9. You can have a piece of candy once you have finished your lunch.

________________ 10. We are watching the game while we wait for our table to be ready.

________________ 11. Marie will either eat with her mom, or she will go to the restaurant by herself.

________________ 12. We tried to get tickets to the concert, yet we failed.

EXERCISE 79

Q147] Fill in the blanks using correlative conjunctions. Use each pair only once:

neither - nor   whether - or   either - or   both - and   as - as   not - but   not only - but also

(A)

1. The teacher __________ left the classroom, __________ slammed the door.
2. __________ my mom __________ my dad graduated from college.
3. You have to keep the car __________ close to the curb __________ possible.
4. We cannot decide __________ we should go to France __________ Italy.
5. It's __________ about how much money you have __________ how you spend it.
6. __________ my cousin __________ my grandma love to eat shrimp and grits.

(B)

1. He has to decide __________ to go to college _____ get a job.
2. __________ my teacher __________ my principal has met my mom.
3. We found __________ shells __________ pebbles at the beach.
4. She has __________ talent __________ a solid work ethic.
5. I have to __________ clean my room __________ do the dishes.
6. She is __________ upset __________ not happy.

(C)

1. The waitress was __________ friendly ____________ efficient.
2. ______________ the museum ________________ the school will be closed this Monday.
3. She needs to decide ______________ to cook dinner ________________ to eat at the restaurant.
4. ______________ the dog ______________ the cat ate anything out of the dishes.
5. We can go ______________ to the market ______________ the library.
6. I can ______________ hop on one foot ______________ do a cartwheel.

EXERCISE 80

Q148] Fill in the blanks with appropriate conjunctions.

(i) We started early ______________ we might not miss the show. (because/ so that / on condition that)

(ii) I can help you ____________ you tell me the truth. (so / provided / unless)

(iii) He is both scholarly ______________ cultured. (also / as well / and / as well as)

(iv) He looks ______________ he is ill. (like / as / though / as if)

(v) You must apologize; ______________ you will be punished. (unless / whether / but / otherwise)

(vi) He tiptoed into the class ______________ he should disturb the students. (if / unless / lest)

(vii) ______________ she was angry, she said nothing. (Though / If / Even if)

(viii) We were tired ______________ we had been running for hours. (so / because / while)

Q149] Write the correct conjunction.

1) I need to work hard _______________ I can pass the exam.

2) _______________ he was the best candidate, he didn't win the elections.

3) _______________ you come back from your trip, we'll meet to discuss the problem.

4) They said that movie was fantastic, _______________ I watched it.

5) _______________ he was very ill, he didn't take any medicine

6) I don't know _______________ I can buy a pair of jeans.

7) She went to the shops _______________ couldn't find anything that could fit her needs.

8) Everybody likes him because he is nice _______________ helpful.

9) _______________ he was angry with her, he didn't utter a word.

10) Keep quiet _______________ go out.

Q150] Fill in the blanks with the correct conjunctions.

(i) Nitin had lost his way home _______________ he was not scared. (and / but)

(ii) He knew he was in the woods _______________ he could hear the sound of some wolves howling. (as / and)

(iii) His legs began to hurt _______________ he kept walking. (but/or) The road forked into two narrow paths.

(iv) He could – go left _______________ right. (either – or/ neither – nor) He wondered which road would lead him to his village. He saw that one of the paths looked more worm out than the other.

(v) It had less grass growing. _______________ it also had imprints of footsteps. (or/and)

(vi) Nitin was confident that this path would lead him to his village _______________ people must have walked on it. (because / or)

(vii)   With hope in his heart, Nitin began walking on the chosen path ________________ within half an hour he could see smoke rising into the sky. (but/ and)

(viii)   He was delighted ______________ fire smoke indicated that there were people close by. (but / because)

(ix)   Nitin was so excited that ______________ his legs were aching, he began running. (because/ although)

13

INTERJECTIONS

Interjections are small words that bear no grammatical connection with the sentences in which they are used. They express the emotions or sentiments of the speaker or convey hesitation or protest. They are usually followed by an exclamation mark (or comma).

Since many interjections are mainly written forms of actual sounds that were produced by humans, they are hardly used in academic or scholarly writing, unless they are a part of a direct quote or otherwise.

- *Ah! Now that's what I call a good shot! **Bravo!***

Both **Ah** and **Bravo** are interjections used to show the speaker's admiration in the sentence. There are many different uses for various interjections; the following is a list of the common interjections you may hear around you in daily life

List of Interjections & Examples

Interjection	Interjection Meaning	Interjection Examples
Aah	Exclamation of fear	Aah! The monster's got me!
Ahh	Realization or acceptance	Ahh, now I see what you mean.
Aww	Something sweet or cute	Aww! Just look at that kitten.
Bingo	Acknowledge something as right	Bingo! That's exactly what we were looking for!
Eh	Question something	So that was all she said, eh?

Interjection	Interjection Meaning	Interjection Examples
Eww	Something disgusting	Eww! That movie was so gory.
Hmph	To indicate displeasure	Hmph. I could do that for half the amount he charged.
Oh	I see/ I think	Oh, it's been around a week since I saw her.
Oops	Making a mistake	Oops! Sorry I didn't see those skates there.
Ouch	Exclamation of pain	Ouch, that hurt! Stop pinching me!
Shh	An indication for silence	Shh! The show is about to start.
Uh oh	Showing dismay	Uh oh! The teacher's caught him.
Whew	Amazement and/or relief	Whew! I can't believe we actually finished it all.
Wow	Expressing surprise or admiration	Wow! That's really great news!
Yay/Yaay	Congratulatory exclamation	I can't believe you're actually coming here! Yaay!
Yeah	Variant of 'yes'	Yeah, I'd love some orange juice.
Yikes	For fear or concern (not serious)	Yikes, my mother's home!
Yippee	Exclamation of celebration	Yippee! We won, lets head to the bar.

Some interjections are used to stall for time or indicate that the speaker is thinking of something. These interjections are also used when someone doesn't know what to say. The following is a list of these sounds or words; they are also called **Hesitation Devices:**

Interjection	Interjection Meaning	Interjection Examples
Uh	Indicates a pause/ need for more time	Wait I know this... uh... is it Ruskin Bond?

Hmm	Thinking/Hesitating about something	Hmm, I'm not sure this colour is the best for this room.
Er	Not knowing what to say	I don't think...er... wait... let me call my boss.
Um	Pausing or being skeptical	Not that I don't believe you but, um, you say it's a ghost?

TYPES OF INTERJECTIONS

Type of Interjection	Definition	Example
Joyful Interjections	Express excitement or happiness.	• Hooray! • Yay!
Surprised Interjections	Express disbelief or amazement	• Oh my goodness! • Wow!
Exclamatory Interjections	Express reactions or emotions	• Bravo!
Conversational Interjections	Used in informal communication	• Well • Anyway
Positive Interjections	Convey positive emotions	• Yippee! • Fantastic!
Negative Interjections	Convey negative emotions.	• Ouch! • Ugh!
Casual Interjections	Used casually	• Uh-huh • Hmm
Formal Interjections	Used formally	• Alas! • Indeed!
Mild Interjections	Express moderate emotions	• Hmm • Well
Strong Interjections	Express intense emotions	• Yikes! • Wow!
Expressive Interjections	Adding emotion to statements	• Ah! • Oh!
Attention-Grabbing Interjections	Capturing someone's focus	• Hey! • Listen!
Interruptive Interjections	Used to interrupt a conversation	• Stop! • Wait!
Responsive Interjections:	Used while responding to something	• Oh, I see! • Really!

EXERCISE 81

Q151] (A) Underline the interjections in the following sentences.

1. Super! I'm excited to go to the party with you!
2. Yippee! It's finally summer vacation!
3. Oh no! I left my baseball glove at the field.
4. Oh, I completely forgot to tell you about the test tomorrow.
5. Gosh, I can't believe I forgot to do my homework.
6. Alas, we have to stop playing and start studying.

(B) Replace the interjection with one that makes more sense. Write the new interjection on the line.

_______Yes!_______ 1. Oh no! I won the contest!

_________________ 2. Yay! We lost the game.

_________________ 3. Ugh. This is the best day ever!

_________________ 4. No! I am so excited to go to this concert!

_________________ 5. Yuck! This meal is so delicious.

_________________ 6. Nice work! You did a horrible job on your test.

Q152] (A)Underline the interjections in the following sentences.

1. Yummy! This is my favorite dessert!
2. Yikes! That spider is so scary!
3. Ugh. I hate when I forget my homework.
4. Oh no! I missed the bus!
5. Sorry, I cannot make it to the party.
6. No! Say it isn't true!

(B)Replace the interjection with one that makes more sense. Write the new interjection on the line.

__Woohoo!__ 1. Ouch! What a great party!

_________________ 2. Oh no! I got the highest score on the test.

_________________ 3. Yummy! This hamburger meat is rotten.

_________________ 4. Way to go! Your team lost the game.

_________________ 5. Boo! This movie is the best movie ever.

_________________ 6. Bravo! Please stop singing this awful song.

EXERCISE 82

Q154] Rewrite each sentence with an interjection to add excitement and drama.

(A) 1. That magic trick is amazing!

Unbelievable! That magic trick is amazing!

2. I fell over and ripped my pants.

____

3. This is the exact shirt I wanted to get!

____

4. Sometimes life is tougher than I'd like it to be.

____

5. I had no idea you were related to my family!

____

6. This cake is the most delicious dessert ever!

____

7. I cannot attend your wedding this summer.

____

8. I forgot to bring the birthday present.

____

(B) 1. We finally won a contest!

Woohoo! We finally won a contest!

2. You are going to get to attend the festival!

____

3. That spaghetti sauce has ants in it!

____

4. This is the wrong phone number.

____

5. What an awesome show!

____

6. I do not want to go back to school after spring break.

____

7. That flu shot really hurts.

____

8. I left my luggage at the airport!

____

(C) 1. That's awful to hear!

No! That's awful to hear!

2. That is exactly what I was thinking!

____

3. I'm so excited to be at the amusement park today!

____

4. I can't believe I forgot to call her on her birthday!

____

5. I can't help you out tomorrow.

____

6. That's the most disgusting thing I've ever seen!

____

7. I'm so bored in this class.

____

8. This is the best day ever!

____

EXERCISE 83

Mild interjections (*Yeah, ...*) show little emotion and are separated from the rest of the sentence with a comma.

Strong interjections (*Yippee!, ...*) show a lot of emotion and are separated from the rest of the sentence with an exclamation mark.

Q155] (A) Circle the interjection in each sentence. Circle mild or strong to identify the type of interjection.

__strong__ 1. Gee! What a fabulous idea!

_________ 2. Yuck! This tastes disgusting.

_________ 3. Congratulations! You got the job.

_________ 4. Well, we can study tonight or tomorrow.

_________ 5. Wow! What a great play by the catcher!

__________ 6. Yes, we are going to the play tomorrow.

__________ 7. Oh no! He was in a car accident!

__________ 8. Uh, I thought this was the right house, but now I'm not so sure.

(B) __strong__ 1. Wow! What an awesome painting!

__________ 2. Yes, we can come to the party tonight.

__________ 3. Hello! How are you?

__________ 4. Goodness! That was a very long speech!

__________ 5. Well, you look very handsome this evening.

__________ 6. Alas, we had to make a very tough decision.

__________ 7. No! You cannot run around the house and chase your brother!

__________ 8. Great! I've always wanted to visit this restaurant!

(C) __mild__ 1. Gee, I hadn't thought of that.

__________ 2. Well, you can ask your friend for advice.

__________ 3. Ouch! I stubbed my toe!

__________ 4. Yippee! We won our first game!

__________ 5. Oh! You forgot to call me back.

__________ 6. Ugh, I cannot wait for this class to end.

__________ 7. Oh no! I missed the bus this morning!

__________ 8. Yuck! I think this meal is disgusting

EXERCISE 84

Q156] In the following sentences, identify the interjection and underline it.

   (i)   Hi, I glad that you could make it to my party

   (ii)   Wow! You look great tonight.

   (iii)   That was the best performance that I have ever seen, bravo!

   (iv)   I can't believe you broke my favourite toy, bah.

   (v)   Hmm, I wonder where I put my keys and wallet?

   (vi)   Miners used to shout, eureka, when they struck gold.

   (vii)   "Shoo!" shouted the woman when she saw the cat licking milk from her cereal bowl.

   (viii)   I guess that's the end of the movie, darn.

   (ix)   Stop! You should always wear a helmet when riding a bike.

   (x)   Yippee, I made this picture all by myself.

EXERCISE 85

Q157] Add an interjection to each sentence.

   (i)   ___________ ! Do not interrupt the teacher.

   (ii)   ___________ what a wonderful time we had at the mall!

   (iii)   ___________ this is an awesome microwavable dinner

   (iv)   ___________ what a fabulous experience for students.

   (v)   ___________ ! So you have finally decided to go.

   (vi)   ___________ ! what an incredibly rude thing to say!

   (vii)   ___________ ! I can't take it anymore.

   (viii)   ___________ ! you look great in those clear heels!

   (ix)   ___________ The police are coming

   (x)   ___________ the earth is shaking!

Q158] Make appropriate sentences using the following interjections.

   1. Alas

____

2. Yeah,

____

3. Great

____

4. Eh!

____

5. Ugh!

____

6. Stop!

____

7. Wow!

____

8. Yes!

____

9. What!

____

Q159] Fill in the blanks appropriate interjections.

1.   .... We have a party tomorrow!
2.   .... You look great this morning.
3.   .... That was the best performance to date.
4.   .... I can't believe you broke my favorite toy.
5.   .... I think I have lost my keys again.
6.   .... I finally finished the painting.
7.   .... J. K. Rowling is doing a reading at the local library.
8.   .... What a pretty dress!
9.   .... That feels good.
10. .... That hurts!

PUNCTUATIONS

A punctuation mark is a character used to punctuate, that is, to separate, elements of writing, such as sentences or phrases. Using punctuation is vital to make your writing look professional, logical and well-founded. Using no punctuation at all will not make sense; overuse of punctuation can make your writing look distorted and vague.

Punctuation mark	Symbols	Uses	Sentence example
Full stop / Period	.	There are two most common uses of a full stop: to indicate the end of a sentence, or to follow an abbreviation.	I am a teacher. 'ft.' is an abbreviation of foot.
Comma	,	A comma is often used to separate different ideas in a sentence. However, it has many other uses as well.	Hello, good morning!
Colon	:	It can introduce an example, a list, an explanation, or a quotation. Or, can also use it to emphasize	You have two choices: run away or fight.

Punctuation mark	Symbols	Uses	Sentence example
Semicolon	;	A semicolon is a punctuation mark that creates a longer pause than a comma but a shorter pause than a full stop. So, it can be used to create a pause between two independent clauses that are still closely related to each other.	I did not like the dish; however, I ate it since I did not want to waste it.
Apostrophe	'	An apostrophe has two very important uses. Firstly, it can be used in contractions in place of omitted letters. Secondly, it can show possession.	-This is Sanjana's mansion. -Aren't, here apostrophe denotes omission of letter 'o' in 'are not'.
Single Quotation marks	'..........'	Are used to indicate dialogue within another quotation.	Aditi asked, "Did you say, 'I don't want to go'? "
Double Quotation marks	'..........'	As their name suggests, quotation marks indicate direct quotation. You can also use them to show that a word or a phase is being used ironically or for titles of articles, book chapters, episodes of a TV-show, etc.	-My dad said, "Make sure you get home before 8 p.m." -The title of the chapter, "The Enemy".
Hyphen	–	It's mostly used to create compound words.	We have a blue-eyed Persian cat.

Punctuation mark	Symbols	Uses	Sentence example
Dash	—	There are two different dashes, the first being slightly shorter than the second one. The en dash is usually used to show a connection between two things, as well as a range of numbers, years, pages, etc.	My mom's friends — Sheela and Agnes — visited her today.
Parentheses	(......)	In most cases, you will see additional information in parentheses. Usually, it can be omitted without creating any confusion for the reader.	SRK (Shah Rukh Khan) is the King of Bollywood.
Square Bracket	[......]	Brackets are, in a way, similar to parentheses. However, they are mostly in academic writing and when presenting quotes. For instance, the writer can add extra information or fix mistakes in brackets, without changing the original quotation.	"A meal at that restaurant will cost you $100 [90 euros]."
Slash	/	You might need to write a fraction, a measurement, or to suggest alternatives in your text.	You can have pizza/burger in the evening snacks.

Punctuation mark	Symbols	Uses	Sentence example
Exclamation mark	!	An exclamation mark added at the end of a sentences shows emphasis. Depending on the meaning of the sentences, it can indicate anger, happiness, excitement, or any other strong emotion.	Wow! It is so mesmerizing.
Question mark	?	A question mark, as its name suggests, needs to go at the end of every interrogative sentence instead of a full stop.	What would you like to have for dinner?
Ellipsis	...	An ellipsis creates an intriguing and mysterious atmosphere in the text. In additional, it can be used to show that some letters or even words are omitted.	We wrote in the comments section, "We were here. This is the ... again."
Asterisk	*	Most commonly used to signal a footnote, but sometimes also used to clarify a statement or censor inappropriate language.	*All contestants should be above 18 years of age.

SECTION B

SPOKEN ENGLISH

15

SPOKEN ENGLISH & ITS IMPORTANCE

English being accepted as the global language, in order to maintain international relationship in science, technology, business, education, travel, tourism and so on, English serves the purpose as a common language and a global language. It is the language mostly used not only by the business organizations and the internet but also in higher education, and tourism sectors. As English plays a dominant role in almost all the fields in the present globalized world, there is a need to discuss its role as a global language. The significance of English as a global language is next level as most of the world's communications is done in English. English is being widely used in scientific research, business and education. Several other sectors like travel and tourism, entertainment fields, and employment are benefitted by adopting English as their principal language of communication. Introduction With the ever-growing levels of interconnectivity and globalization around the world, the significance of immediate and appropriate modes of communication has been increasing very rapidly in this modern world. It is an undeniable fact that there is a need for a common language to communicate with the present growing commerce and trade between companies from all over the world. With the development of informatization as well as globalization, it is evident that most people all over the world are communicating with the people of other regions in only one internationally recognized language, that is, English. English is the language that is almost used between an agent and an international company. English, being the first world language, is said to be the first global lingua franca and it is the most widely used language in the world in international trade, diplomacy, mass entertainment, international telecommunications and scientific publications as well as publishing newspapers and other books. Learning English, spoken more than written brings you a lot of opportunities in education as well as employment sector. Speaking English is not a want but a need in today's modern world.

16

IMPORTANT TIPS

How to learn English fast and effectively ?

1. Surround yourself with English

- Talk to native English speakers every day.
- Find a language exchange group to practice speaking with other learners.
- Participate in cultural events and social gatherings where English is spoken.
- Try to practice speaking English in front of a mirror, or you can also try recording yourself to improve your pronunciation.
- Get involved in English group discussions and debates.

2. Practice active listening

If you want to communicate effectively in English, you need to have good listening skills. It's a crucial part of **learning English**. By listening attentively, you can enhance your English-speaking abilities and expand your vocabulary and grammar with new words.

- Watch English movies, TV shows, and videos with subtitles to improve your vocabulary and cultural knowledge while getting entertained.
- Listen to English language podcasts, news, and radio to enhance your listening ability, pronunciation, and fluency.
- Discover different accents and dialects to get comfortable with English quickly.

- Engage in conversations with native English speakers to practice your listening skills in a natural setting.
- Don't just hear it; actively listen! Pay attention to the speaker and ask questions. By doing so, you'll be able to respond appropriately and contribute meaningfully to conversations.

Note: Active listening is an essential part of learning English.

3. Read, read, read!

- Pick books that interest you, such as novels, thrillers, or non-fiction. Choose what captures your attention to stay motivated and engaged.
- Start with shorter texts like articles, short stories, or children's books to build confidence and understanding of the language.
- Read aloud to practice pronunciation and intonation and to train your brain to process spoken English.
- Note down atleast 5-10 new vocabulary words daily and go through it daily unless your brain stores it permanently. Use those words while speaking daily somehow, somewhere which will help you memorize faster and let you know where to use the word exactly while speaking.

4. Writing practise

Writing is a fantastic way to get better at English! Not only can you practice using new words and **learn English grammar**, but it also improves your critical thinking and helps you express your thoughts better. Besides, writing is everywhere these days - from emails to social media posts to essays, whether for school or work, writing is essential. By practising your writing, you'll be able to communicate with confidence and get your message across clearly.

- Start small and simple. Begin with short sentences and easy-to-understand paragraphs to feel more confident and less overwhelmed.

- Writing is a skill, and it takes practice. So, make sure to write regularly, even if it's just a few sentences each day.
- Get feedback from someone you trust. Ask them to read your writing and give you their honest opinion. This way, you'll be able to identify areas where you can improve and build on your strengths.

With these writing tips and regular practice, becoming a fluent English writer will be a breeze! So, gather your pens and paper to start writing your way to fluency!

5. Learn English speaking through daily practice

Daily Practice is the key if you want to become a confident English speaker! It'll help you sound more natural, improve your vocabulary, and get comfortable talking to native speakers. **Learn English speaking** by talking to people who speak English fluently in a natural setting.

- Listening to English speakers and repeating what they do to improve your pronunciation and fluency.
- Recording yourself speaking in English to identify the areas that need improvement. You can also monitor your progress over time and see how much you have improved.
- Practice makes perfect! Make an effort to speak English every day, even if it's just for 15 minutes.
- Don't be afraid to make mistakes! **Learning English** can be challenging, but the more you practice, the better you'll become.
- There are many innovative ways to practice speaking English, like storytelling, poetry, enrolling in **English courses** or attending stand-up comedy workshops. Try different methods to keep it fun and engaging!

6. Build your English vocabulary bank

Building up your vocabulary in English is a game-changer. The words you know shape the way you express yourself, so the more words you know, the better you can express yourself and communicate with others.

- Read more books, articles, and newspapers to discover new words and write down unfamiliar words to look up their meanings later.
- Play word games like crossword puzzles and word searches to reinforce your vocabulary.
- Keep a vocabulary journal to track your progress and learn new words.
- Quiz yourself regularly using flashcards to memorise new words.
- Use new words in everyday conversations and writing to improve your English skills.
- Stick a label with the English name on everyday objects like a chair, table, or computer and say it aloud whenever you see it. This is a creative way to learn the English names of everyday objects.

7. Learn English grammar rules

Learning English grammar can be challenging, but it's achievable with the right approach. In this book, we have compiled very selective data and created the grammar section in the easiest possible way. I assure, the grammar topics covered in this book are enough to learn writing and speaking English in a ready-to-go manner.

- Start with the basics, verb tenses, pronouns, and sentence structure.
- Practice tongue twisters to improve your pronunciation and grammar.
- Try using grammar checker tools to help identify areas that need improvement.
- Don't be afraid to ask for help. You can enrol yourself in Rai's Academy for learning English effectively.

8. Start thinking in English

The more English you see and hear around you, the easier it will be to start **learning English**.

- Change your phone and computer settings to English, listen to English music and podcasts, and watch English movies and TV shows. Slowly, your brain will get used to processing the language, and you'll start to find yourself thinking in English more naturally.

- Practice with simple sentences initially.
- Try to use English in your daily life as much as possible. Even simple activities like doing household chores or making a grocery list can be a chance to think in English.
- Start with a list of things around yourself: vegetables, fruits, household articles, body parts, body habits.
- It's okay to make mistakes. In fact, it's a natural part of the learning process. So, feel free to try new words or phrases, even if you're unsure if they're correct.

9. Learning English with translation technique

- When translating texts, don't just copy-paste the translation. Instead, try to paraphrase the text in your own words while still maintaining its meaning.
- If you're watching movies or TV shows in English, turn on the subtitles in your native language. This will help you understand the dialogues better.
- Don't just translate English to your native language, but also try translating your native language to English to understand how words and phrases are used in different contexts.
- As you translate, pay close attention to the grammar and sentence structure of the text. This will help you improve your own grammar and sentence construction in English.
- Practice translating daily to develop a consistent routine and track your progress.
- Use translation software like Google Translate to get started and then review and revise your translations on your own.

10. Public Speaking

Public speaking is an art which needs a lot of confidence. Several people deal with stage fear and nervousness. For overcoming stage fear, regular practice is needed in order to boost confidence. Having a good command over grammar boosts confidence in the individual automatically.

- Start speaking in front of family and friends.
- Indulge in group discussions.
- For overcoming fear, atleast you need to start from somewhere.
- Keep practicing, it's the only key to reach accuracy.

11. Enrol in Rai Academy's English courses.

Rai Academy is specially for **the Beginners** who desire to learn spoken and writing English effectively irrespective of their age. One can start learning English at any stage of life. Rai Academy provides English Speaking courses as well as Personality development courses. It provides **personalized learning.** To get modules for learning spoken English and grammar, one can contact us at sanjurai2607@gmail.com and let us know their need regarding English.

LEARNING SPOKEN ENGLISH AND GRAMMAR

MADE EASY AND FUN.

HAPPY LEARNING!